FEILD NOTES

The Brothers with their parents. (Left to right) William Presley Feild, William "Will" H. Feild, Jr., Joseph, Mary Rebecca, and Ernest Feild, circa 1865

Feild Notes on Little Rock

History and Memoir
1622–2024

I *before* E
Unless It Is Me

Charles R. Feild, MD MPH

Charles R. Feild, MD MPH
cfeild@swbell.net

ISBN: 978-1-7353167-5-8

Book and cover design: H. K. Stewart

NANDINA BOOKS
Little Rock, Arkansas

Printed in the United States of America

For my daddy *and my* grandson

Feild* Names

*Yes, "I before E." Unless it is me.

In Early Modern English, IE, EI, and E were interchangeable in printed work of the 17th century and in private correspondence of educated people into the 19th century.

I have taken license to standardize the multiple spellings of FEILD when I am certain they are in the FEILD family line. To put I before E is irresistible.

The Main Characters

WILLIAM "RUSH" HUME FEILD, SR.
B: July 1796, Brunswick, Virginia
D: May 1861, Little Rock, Arkansas

WILLIAM "WILL" HUME FEILD, JR.
B: 1827, Pulaski, Tennessee
D: 1861, Little Rock, Arkansas

MARY REBECCA JAMESON FEILD
B: January 1834
D: April 1909

WP and Florence, circa 1920

WILLIAM PRESLEY FEILD, SR.
B: *July 1854, Danville, Arkansas*
D: *May 1921, Memphis, Tennessee*

FLORENCE HUNTER FIELD
B: *1956, Tulip, Arkansas*
D: *1920, Little Rock, Arkansas*

ERNEST JAMESON FEILD
B: *September 1856, Danville, Arkansas*
D: *April 1924, Little Rock, Arkansas*
Photo circa 1890

JOSEPH HAROLD FEILD
B: *September 1859, Danville, Arkansas*
D: *May 1921, Little Rock, Arkansas*
Only known photo, circa 1865

Pappaw and Mater, circa 1917

RUSSELL HUNTER FEILD, SR.	MARY BERNARD MILLS FEILD
B: 1888, Little Rock, Arkansas	B: 1894, Little Rock, Arkansas
D: 1969, Little Rock, Arkansas	D: 1968, Little Rock, Arkansas

Daddy and Mama, circa 1945

ROBERT MILLS FEILD	IRENE ELIZABETH EDWARDS FEILD
B: 1920, Little Rock, Arkansas	B: 1921, Bald Knob, Arkansas
D: 2002, Little Rock, Arkansas	D: 2014, Little Rock, Arkansas

CHARLES ROBERT FEILD
B: 1953, Little Rock, Arkansas

Contents

INTRODUCTION

This is not a Feild genealogy. A 1901 two-volume tome* was compiled 120 years closer to the source materials than present day. My purpose is to take the stories of multiple generations of one family—mine—and to inform history now, and for folks that follow.

My daddy could turn family stories of 50 or 150 years ago into real people, places, and events as if they happened just the other day and make the long dead seem as if they just walked out of the room to soon return. When my son was 10 years old, he told me matter-of-factly what he and Daddy talked about. "Oh, you know, the war and how things used to be," melding generations and centuries again.

Mama kept old newspapers in a woven basket. As her powers slipped, I by chance took the loaded basket home to recycle. As I pulled out stacks of old *Democrat Gazettes*, I found underneath a mess of past-due notices, unpaid bills, and unopened correspondence—termite contract, lawn service, Medicare, doctor's and clinic bills. I sat on the floor with a pile of old newspapers, unmet obligations, and windowed envelopes, and made a close inspection of the basket. My wife said, "Oh, that's the basket from The Farm."

*Pierce, Frederick Clifton. *Field [sic] genealogy: being the record of all the Field [sic] family in America, whose ancestors were in this country prior to 1700: Volume II*. Chicago: W.B. Conkey, 1901.

Somehow, I missed the origin story that Mama shared with her. The basket was crafted on Feild Bros Farm, reportedly by a former slave, to hold my daddy after his 1921 birth. Like Mama, it was very fragile. I took it to the Historic Arkansas Museum for an expert opinion on the origin, and donate it for preservation in a controlled environment. As I talked to curator Hattie Felton, I spouted some of my accumulated lore. She told me, "Write this down. The stories. Other people will do genealogy."

I realized I had a trove of old photos, letters, clippings, and ephemera that had been passed on by generations and by decade and century, a large jumble never studied, to go with Daddy's stories, facts, and perhaps a few myths.

I have 64 great-great-great-grandparents. I am but a tiny bit of DNA from each of them, my 1/64th Feild DNA is no more special than anyone else's. Thanks to Mama and Daddy, much assistance, and pure-dee luck, I do have most names and many faces.

Since this project began, public discussions have distorted the past, the truth, of chattel slavery, the Civil War, Jim Crow, and the Lost Cause. The truth is characterized as wokeness (sic) and indoctrination. Additions have been made to the initial draft, local people and stories, and local truths. Thanks to resources of the Central Arkansas Library System, first-person voices of Freedmen can be shared for the first time.

This has brought new friends, and help from strangers. Hattie Felton is now Director of Curatorial Affairs & Curator of Fine and Decorative Arts at the Missouri Historical Society. Special thanks to Brian Robertson of the Central Arkansas Library System's Roberts Library for coming to our house and looking through stacks of papers and pictures from Pappaw and Mater's attic; Rhonda Stewart of Roberts Library for help with writing on enslaved and Freedmen; Mike Hood, former chief civil engineer with the City of Little Rock; Dr Brian Mitchell formerly of the University of Arkansas at Little Rock and now Research Director, Lincoln

Museum and Library, Springfield Illinois; Carla Coleman of the Arkansas Black History Commission; neighbor Frances Carner whose work is documenting the West Rock community. Jane Jones-Schulz, who questioned and encouraged and read multiple drafts, and corrected my non-existent keyboard skills, spotting inconsistency and redundancy. Most of all she helped by clarifying where I was confusing or overreached trying to be clever. H. K. Stewart has edited for publishing and encouraged for two years.

These are stories, not an academic treatise. I benefit from *The Pulaski County Historical Quarterly*, online sources Library of Congress, ancestry.com, newspapers.com. The JSTOR.org digital made *The Arkansas History Quarterly* and other scholarly sources accessible. The Roberts Library of Arkansas History has provided safe conservation and online access of the Feild Family Papers [https://arstudies.contentdm.oclc.org/digital/collection/findingaids/id/10772/rec/2]

LITTLE ROCK CENSUS

1820 <30
1850 2,167
1860 3,727
1870 12,380
1880 13,138
1890 25,874
1900 38,307
1910 45,941
1920 65,142
1930 81,679
1940 88,039
1950 102,213
1960 107,813
1970 132,483
1980 159,151
1990 175,795
2000 183,133
2010 193,524
2020 202,591

I.

FEILD VERSUS FEILD

"Jarndyce v Jarndyce drones on"
Bleak House, Charles Dickens, 1853

The Feild family had been in Arkansas since 1843, but I begin with the Feild Brothers. They are my great-grandfather William Presley Feild, Sr (1854–1921) and his two brothers Ernest (1865–1924) and Joe (1860–1921) at the family home at 811 Scott Street in Little Rock. Five generations lived and worked there in a rambling frame home. Initially, it occupied the entire east side of Scott Street between 8th and 9th Streets, later enumerated as 811 Scott Street. Known then and now to family simply as 811, it was home and business address.

> Today, Mr. HA Bowman acting as agent, sold 2 acres of land near the Southern Oil Mills, belonging to Feild brothers, to Mr. J Bowman, and another gentleman. It is understood the ground will be used for a lumberyard.
> *Arkansas Democrat*, November 1889

They were simply the Feild Bros or just Bros. The first time local news reported on them in the aggregate was as THE Brothers, no further introduction required. Locals already knew them, in and of Little Rock, for 20 years, and would for the next 30 years. They would all consider themselves farmers, then the more accurate, or only uppity self-proclaimed, planters. The eldest, William Presley Jr., "WP," was the joiner and a leader on business, bank, and civic boards, and a Sunday school superintendent. Ernest enjoyed life as fisherman, a traveler, and a Rooter—a rowdy club of baseball fans. But Uncle Joe, the youngest and the lifelong bachelor, was quiet, a temperance man, rarely in the news. Uncle Joe, 100 years after death, is still known in the family for eccentricity that included a sometimes lack of physical modesty. He spoke the dismissive words still quoted: "Who wants to see a naked man, anyway." In his deshabille, he confused others' embarrassed, averted gaze for disinterest. Ernest's granddaughter Ida Kaufman recalled him as the "black sheep," but she had been a child born after his death and recalls no bill of particulars.

Together, the three were THE Feild Bros to one and all. Their lives bracketed the sleepy, slow paced time pre-Civil War to the Roaring Twenties. A century ago, a 1921 January sentence in the paper noted that Ernest, age 65, was ill at home. Whatever his problem or setback, he recovered with no further public notice taken.

"E. J. Feild, Sr., is confined to his bed at 811 Scott Street as the result of a setback suffered by him during the past week."
Daily News, January 1921

The *Arkansas Gazette* reported the same, in small town fashion, quaintly publishing folks' doings—the white folks, male mostly, but also women. No news was too trivial, their socializing, comings and goings, for hotels and riverboats, visiting and visitors, and illnesses. For African Americans, only the occasional line or two, "colored," "negro/ negress," never the honorifics of Mr. or Miss/Mrs.

The Bros' mother, Florence, had died with tuberculosis just before New Year's Eve 1920. My Feild grandparents, Russell/Pappaw and Mary Bernard/Mater were living with Mater's parents, the Mills, and getting help with their first baby. Later that month, they presented W. P. with his second grandson, Robert, my daddy.

The Feild Bros' multiple enterprises continued as usual—cotton, banking, local business investment, and buying, selling, renting property, farmland and residential. From 1911, this included the new residential blocks in the Feild's Addition two miles due west, near the State Lunatic Asylum. They had around 10 square miles of land including farmlands on both sides of the Arkansas River. And the jewel in the crown, referred to then and now by family, was THE Farm—1,400 prime acres hugging the river just north and west of the city (My Pappaw had assumed day-to-day Farm operations). In March of 1921, the Bros, as "Heirs and Living Relatives of William H. Feild," obtained a Duplicate Swamp Land Certificate (the 1854 original lost) for 80 acres in Yell County, tidying up the title for subsequent owners. Two blocks away, First Methodist Episcopal Church–South, or First Church, was part of daily life for all three Bros. Will, Pappaw, Daddy, me, my offspring, and now my grandson, all have attended there. WP, a recent widower, was 67 years old.

He paid a visit to the Memphis home of his one daughter, Kathleen Feild Tobey, Aunt Kathleen (1885–1965). He made the trip just fine, but on May 8, he died there in his sleep at her home. His obituary mentioned he had been ill since Florence's death. He was buried at Mount Holly cemetery, with First Methodist Episcopal Church–South's entire Board of Stewards as well as the Board of Trustees serving as dozens of honorary pallbearers. Then Uncle Joe died just two weeks later on May 23, 1921, at age 63 at nephew Presley, Jr.'s, home. Unlike WP's large crowd, a small funeral conducted there. Pallbearers included WP's brother-in-law.

Ernest, whose wife had died in 1918, was the sole surviving bro. The family and the town expected the bachelor uncle's will would divide his estate among his family.

The actual newspaper report:

FEILD LEAVES ENTIRE ESTATE TO FOUR INSTITUTIONS
By the will of the late Joseph H. Feild of Little Rock ...four
Arkansas educational and charitable institutions are made the
sole beneficiary of Mr. Feild's estate, estimated at $50,000.
Hendrix College of Conway will receive 40 percent, the
Arkansas Methodist Orphanage will receive 30 percent, the
Ada Thompson home will receive 20 percent, and the
Florence Crittenden home will get 10 percent. By the terms
of the will dated December 27, 1918, all of Mr. Feild's
property, real and personal, is to be sold after all debts are
met, and the money invested in United States Bonds ....
[Survivors] are Ernest J. Feild, two nieces, Mrs. Eloise Feild
Weir and Miss Kathleen Feild Tobey; and three nephews, W.
P. Feild, Jr., R. H. Feild, and E. J. Feild, Jr. Much of the estate
is in real estate in Little Rock, and the Feild brothers farm of
1,200 acres five miles north of Little Rock. The property has
not been divided, and for this reason the exact amount of
the estate of J. H. Feild has not been made public.
Little Rock Daily News, May 28, 1921

The beneficences were in honor of his parents, his mother's
memorials to Florence Crittenden Home and Ada Thompson
Home, and for his father, Hendrix, and the Orphanage. For the
living relations, not a cent, not even a mention. Reading between
the lines, the *News* recognized this as unexpected and as newsworthy. The surviving family lawyered up.

WARNING ORDER
State of Arkansas, County of Pulaski, W. P. Feild et al Plaintiff
vs Ernest J. Feild et al \\Defendant in the Pulaski Chancery
Court-No 27758

> The Defendant, Forney Hutchinson as executor of the will of
> Joseph H. Field, is warned to appear in this court and
> answer the complainant of the Plaintiff W. P. Feild et al.
> June 8, 1921

> included "approximately 6,205 acres of land, including the
> 1,105.5-acre plantation north of Little Rock, which is valued
> at $21,200" ($281,000 in 2021).

Almost 10 square miles were the holdings of the Bros, but the Bros were no more.

ESTATE IS APPRAISED
The Report Is Filed In Suit To Change J. H. Feild Will
The report of the appraisers appointed by Chancellor Martineau was filed yesterday in the suit of W. P. Feild, Kathleen Feild Tobey, and Russell H. Feild, against the executors and trustees of the will of the late Joseph H. Field who bequeathed almost his entire estate to charity. The suit is an attempt on the part of the natural heirs-at-law to have these dispositions changed so that they may share in the estate. Real estate holdings of the deceased were valued at $172,267.25 by the appraisers R. W. Polk, John H. Hollis, and Bodeman.
Daily Arkansas Gazette, September 1922

In current dollars, this initial estimate conservatively equals $2.5 million. In October, Ernest petitioned to be added to the court case. The process was long, but never got better. The last court entry was in 1960. An error in the legal description of a property in the appraisal was noted and corrected, at the cost of $1.50. In a later chapter, the end of the end will prove to be even later.

The will was airtight. The relations got what Uncle Joe intended. The judgement, May 1923, gave three equal shares, each valued $50,399 (2021 $780,000), to Uncle Joe's bequests. Ernest and WP's heirs—Presley, Kathleen, and Pappaw—were left to divide the remainder. The jewel, The Farm, Feild Bros Farm, was divided three ways in the midst of plummeting market prices. Pappaw had attended University of Arkansas for two years to study agriculture and had been running the farm since 1918. He was left with only one-ninth of his beloved lands, now a rapidly declining asset. It ain't *Jarndyce v Jarndyce*, but similar twists and turns have followed descendants.

II.

THE FEILD BROS FARM

Along the south bank of the Arkansas River, downstream from the Big Dam Bridge stretching over Murray Lock and Dam, is a two-mile stretch of preserved wetlands, stands of timber, and public parkland. From 1898, The Feild/Feilds/Field/Fields/Bros/Bros Farm was for the family simply "The Farm," and even today over 100 years later, it's still "The Farm." Amid massive cottonwoods, sweetgum, oaks, willows, cypress, cane breaks, and swampland were a pecan grove, wells, and commissary. The sharecropper family housing had plots for poultry, swine, and vegetables, and some rented a few additional acres for corn. At times there was a steam-engine-powered cotton gin, a school, and a church. Crime, births, and deaths were recorded and reported in newspapers as occurring at "Feilds' Farm."

BIRTHS
To Mr. and Mrs. J.H. Rice, 902 Marshall Street,
September 7, a son.
Negroes: To Toma and George Caloway, Feilds' Farm,
July 13, a daughter; to Richard and Lula Baily, Feilds' Farm,
November 11, 1917; a daughter; to T.E. and Evaline
Williams, Feilds' Farm, August 11, a son; to Abe and Peary

Wyet, Feild's Farm, May 11, a daughter.
Arkansas Democrat, September 1918

From at least 1855, it had been owned by the Greathouse and then Ward families. Cleared and farmed, it functioned as a community:

School Teacher WANTED
The undersigned wants a school teacher in the county, five miles west of Little Rock immediately on the south bank of the River. Liberal wages will be given.
J. Greathouse
True Democrat, March 1856

There were children, Stephen and Bill among them, who would not be educated by the teacher, if one was found.

Notice
Will be sold at public auction, at the courthouse door, in the City of Little Rock, on the first Monday in January 1858, for cash in hand, five slaves, to wit: Hannah, aged 22 years; Stephen, six years; Bill, four years; Molly, two years; Aby, six months. Said slaves belonged to the estate of John J. Rankin, deceased. John Greathouse, Administrator of the estate of J. J. Rankin, deceased.
True Democrat, November 1857

Draining and clearing to yield tillable acreage took time.

I have about 20 acres of improved bottomland for rent, 5 miles above Little Rock. The land belongs to the estate of J. J. Rankin, dec.
J. Greathouse
True Democrat, February 1859

Subsequently, Zeb Ward owned the property. He also had the lease to operate the state penitentiary, located where the current state capitol stands today.

The farm planted 1,400 acres, more than two square miles of cotton. Cotton is a persnickety plant. It requires plowing to a depth of 14 inches, 80 frost-free days, best between 70-100F, 18 inches of rain, not too much while maturing and none during harvest. A gently sloping planting field is best. Enough deviation of one variable, or small aberrations in multiples, and a crop fails. World cotton markets were even more fickle. At every level, all supported by debt. And the old aphorism is true: debt is to agriculture as a rope is to a hanging.

Along the flat, unpaved road a few hundred yards to the east toward town, the closest neighbors were the West Rock community, real estate developed for and marketed to African American families. Children attended Riverside School (Colored), and multi-generational families walked to the Pilgrim Rest Church. Between West Rock and the farm, there was the Choctaw, Oklahoma, and Gulf Railroad (segregated) depot for passengers and freight. This single-track rail, and the parallel River Pike/Perryville Road connected Little Rock to markets to the west.

For months, in my teens, the relentless 24 hours a day, 7 days a week of the Corps' construction pile drivers, building Arkansas River Lock and Dam #7, were a background rhythm, unless every window was shut. That was tough during unairconditioned summers. Now, instead of the Farm, the Park and Golf Course continue to flood every few years, despite the Corps' ongoing efforts.

Three blocks from my childhood home, 1627 Pine Valley Road in the baby boom development Kingwood subdivision, an old dirt track went from the paved streets of Little Rock down to The Farm. We walked it maybe once a year with Daddy, but new homes closed it at the top and overgrowth and erosion finished the job, no longer distinguishable on the steep hillside.

A hundred years later, the lands of THE Farm still have a single owner. The City of Little Rock has Murray Park and Rebsamen Golf Course. West Rock and Pilgrim Rest are gone, thanks to 1950s racism and profiteering in the guise of urban "renewal." Pilgrim Rest relocated to Confederate Boulevard—a street only recently, and finally, renamed Springer Boulevard for African American physician Dr. Worthy Springer. The West Rock families were smugly "rehoused," and the area was renamed Riverdale, a shopping area, and Allsopp Park, developed for whites only. The depot is long gone. The railroad, still single-track, operates only as far as Danville, 100 miles west.

Stories of 811 are passed on, now spanning eight generations and four centuries, the farm six generations. Today 811 is a parking lot, as is so much of the town of the Bros' lifetimes. Aerial photography suggests the site of the cotton gin and residences on old River Pike, roughly across from the golf course pro shop. A walking inspection with civil engineers from the City of Little Rock found no surface evidence of The Farm.

III.

OUR TAINTED
NOT SAINTED FATHER

The Arkansas stories start with the arrival around 1845 in Little Rock of William Hume (Rush) Feild Sr (1796–1860). The arc from Rush to my grandson is eight generations, so with some stories and a few facts, the previous eight generations are introduced, then excused. There is a florid, but murky, oft-quoted, and thereby august, origin story that posits an Alsatian as founder.

"Hubertus de la Feild...
of the family Comté de la Feld, of Colmar in Alsatia"
Appendix by Henry Marlgate Feild
The Family of Rev. David D. Feild, DD, 1860

He was a Comté, for what is an origin story without nobility. Huburtus missed the 1066 Norman Conquest boat, but did cross the Channel in 1068 CE. Per this hagiography, he seemingly sired every Feild/Field/Feld that arrived on American shores and included not a single horse thief, scoundrel, or murderer. Or maybe one. Or two.

The scion of my American Feilds, Bishop Theophilus Feild (1576–1636), was father of two younger brothers who headed to

Virginia. Born in London, he studied at Cambridge as a sizar—i.e., 16th century equivalent of work/study—as well as being identified as a rowdy.

From 1619, he served as Bishop of Llandaff, and St. David's in Wales, and Hereford. His father, John Feild (1545–1587), was a proto-Copernican astronomer and mathematician, which brought him to the attention of the Privy Council for "lewd and vayne practices of calculating and conjuring," though he avoided prison, or the stake and a bonfire.

Like Pilgrim Fathers, the reason for a Bishop's son to head for uncertain wilds was linked to religion, but not inspiring. Bishop Theophilus had financial ambitions, or as he pled in court, needs, due to a wife and six children. Seeking a more lucrative appointment, he was charged in the House of Commons in 1621, with

He was acquitted by his peers, in the House of Lords. But his actions cost him his ecclesiastical honorific, and labeled with the lesser academic title

He attempted to get into good graces, literally and figuratively, with the established Church if not with God by producing 1624 snoozers such as

"The Earths Encrease. Or, A Communion Cup: Presented to the Kings Most Excellent Majesty for a New-Yeeres Gift: By the Reverend Father in God, the Bishop of Llandaff"
"Parasceue Paschæ: or a Christians' preparation to the worthy receiving of the blessed Sacrament of the Lords Supper. Newly enlarged By the Reverend Father in God, the Bishop of Llandaff"

If there remain concerns about the validity of the F-E-I-LD spelling, the above published spelling, should lay those aside.

Spelling mattered in Latin, in English not so much. In one year in one Parish register, the Bishop's brother was spelled Field, Feild, Feld, Felde, Feilde, and Feelde. Shakespeare, born six years after Theophilus, signed his name phonetically, variously, as "Willm Shakp," "William Shaksper," "Wm Shakspe," "William Shakspeare," "Willm Shakspear," and "By me, William Shakspear."

Myriad reasons to accept uncertainty and the dangers of colonizing existed, but "My tainted not sainted father was a bad Bishop and a worse writer" must be among the less common. The Bishop's second son, William Feild (1598–1658), in 1621 set off on the ship *Charles* for Virginia and the New World. Two years earlier, in 1619, the first enslaved African Americans had arrived in Virginia, the year before the Pilgrims arrived in Massachusetts. The fourth son, James (1604–?), crossed the Atlantic on the likely, not very graceful, *Swan* three years later. Reasons to be in Virginia were varied. The year before James made landfall, the *Swan* passenger manifest included John Pedro, "a neger (sic), age 23." His arrival was involuntary. He was enslaved.

James began his life as a colonist, on Captain Samuel Matthews' Plantation, at the confluence of the James and Warwick Rivers. The colorful Captain distinguished himself twice, as the third husband of one of the first four English women settlers, and for a later voyage back to England to be tried for treason, acquitted, and then return. Dealing with travel formalities required by the Virginia Company, and the whiff of incivility at home, both brothers traveled discretely and cheaply, classified as "servants." King Charles simplified their lives in 1624, dissolving the Company and establishing the Royal Colony of Virginia.

An Anglican Bishop, albeit unsavory, as a forebearer, and a Jamestown connection, helps in documenting ancient lineage to compensate for the stubborn (or correct, take your pick) spelling of F-E-I-L-D.

The year 1622 was bad, a very bad time, with disease and starvation, instead of the gold, the fortune seekers expected. A Jamestown resident wrote back to family in England.

> But my brother and my wyfe are dead aboute a year pass'd, and touchinge the busynesse that I came hither is nothing yett performed, by reason of my sickness & weakness I was not able to travell up and downe the hills and dales of these countries...And thus I comitt you to the Almighty.
> Virginia, 13 January 1622.

It seems he died as well.
James's group brought supplies:

> "MIHELL WILLOCKS AND JOHN SLATER THEIR MUSTER their 2 spouses... SERVANTS JAMES FEILD aged 20 in the Swan 1624, 2 other men and PROVISION: Corne, 9 barrels; Houses, 1. ARMES: Peeces, 3; petronell [long-barrelled pistol], 1; Swords, 2; Coates of Male, 2; Lead, 30 lb.
> 1624 record

Slim pickings for survival in a New World.

William seems to have died without issue. James had two sons, James (ca 1630–1671) and Peter (1642–1707), who left his mark. He married into prominent families (first the Randolphs, then as a widower, the Soanes family) and served two terms in the House of Burgesses. His daughter Mary Feild was grand-mother to Thomas Jefferson.

Tracking the Arkansas family until the birth of the Bros' grandfather Feild in 1796 is confusing, and unimaginative, as male heirs' names for more than a century narrowed. Then to two Theophilus(es) and two James(es). And a distant cousin, Theophilus Agricola Feild III, practiced medicine from 1962 until 2011 in Fort Smith, Arkansas.

By the time France established Arkansas Post in 1686, the three generations of Feilds were established and multiplying in Virginia.

IV.
WESTWARD MOVE

The Bros' great-grandfather James Feild (1768–1800) shifted from Tidewater to frontier. He and his wife, Henrietta née Anderson (1769–1814), married in Brunswick, VA. Brunswick was founded in 1670, the western-most outpost of the Colonial British Army. Rush, the son, (1796–1861) was born 172 years after William and James fled the Bishop, and brought a family to Arkansas. Rush was only eight years old when his father died. He attended College of William and Mary, the first degree-granting law school in America, and at Hampden Sydney College. A highly educated lawyer, it is not known how he came by his nickname Rush.

In Giles County in Middle Tennessee, land had been "ceded" by the Chickasaw, and settlers arrived in 1806, joined by Rush around 1810. From the Census he was accompanied by an enslaved male, identified only as age 14 or younger. The cause of his shift to the frontier is at best speculation. After eight generations, many Feilds, maybe too many, had accumulated in Virginia, the soil there depleted. Why Giles County? There were two other Feilds also there, a physician and the proprietor of the hotel. The records do not reveal which Feild got there first.

Rush lived in the county seat, Pulaski, founded in 1809. A log courthouse was built around 1811. Rush was listed among the first six attorneys in residence. Henry Clay and Thomas Hart Benton, from time to time, practiced in the same court. In 1821 at the first local sitting of Chancery Court, he was second in seniority in the Bar.

> Alfred M Harris and William H Field (sic) Have formed a partnership in the practice of law and will attend to the business of their profession in the circuit court of Lawrence, Giles, Lincoln, and Murray—also in the supreme court at Columbia. Their office is the same which has here been occupied by Alfred M Harris on the west side of the public square, in the town of Pulaski.
> *Nashville Whig*, August 1822

William Flournoy, also an attorney from Kentucky, settled his family there in 1813. In 1821, Rush married Flournoy's granddaughter, Amanda, four months after she turned age 16. Their third son, W. H., Jr., Will, arrived in 1826. Amanda's brother chose to go to the wilds of Louisiana where he was killed while hunting wolves. The wolves' outcome is unknown. Andrew Jackson's homestead, the Hermitage, was 90 miles north of Pulaski. He was President (1829–1837), and Rush, also a Democrat, was elected in 1831 to the State Senate. He, the Flournoys, James Polk, later President, and Archibald Yell, a future Arkansas Governor, were fellow Tennessee Democrats who later became Arkansas-connected. On the frontier, everyone was from somewhere else, excepting Indigenous peoples who were driven off. Jackson, Yell, and Polk were from the Carolinas, Amanda from Kentucky, Rush, and both his state senate predecessor and successor, were all born in Virginia.

As a one-term member of the state senate, 1831–32, he had the temerity to vote to cut judges' salaries. He may have been asked to approach more than one judge's bench to explain his vote on a bill to reduce the salaries of the judges and the Supreme Court to …

> strike out $1000 in order [and] insert $500, which was rejected—Mr. Bradford moved an amendment fixing the salaries of the judges in the circuit court at $1000 which was agreed to: AYES ....12; NOes, ...Feild..., 8 (others)

He was a candidate for re-election in 1833, but one sentence in the newspaper, "William H. Feild (Giles) is no longer a candidate for the Senate," marked the end. President Polk wrote to him, lamenting the decision. The reason may have been the birth and then death of their daughter, Henrietta Maria Feild, and likely poor health of Amanda from childbirth.

Rush and his Democrat politics had a brief stint in the newspaper business, listed as owner/publisher/editor of the *Pulaski Trumpet of Liberty* in 1838, supporting Andrew Jackson, and publisher of the *Pulaski Republican* in 1840, supporting James Polk for President. When Polk died in 1849, Rusk adjourned his court for the day and put into the records a pean to him.

V.

FIRST PRIZE, FIRST ROCK, LITTLE PRIZE, LITTLE ROCK

The Petit Roche, Little Rock, is indeed little, especially compared to the nearby north side Big Rock. But it is very significant for navigation, the first stone outcropping encountered as explorers moved upstream. Perhaps the city would have benefitted from the proud primacy of "First" Rock rather than diminutive Little Rock. There is a reason for a First Prize, a First Place, First Ever rather than a Little Prize, a Little Place, Little Ever. First among many, not Little among many, First in the hearts of his countrymen, not Little in their hearts. Little is not Last, but there is a theme here.

The financial Panic of 1837 began with overextended borrowing, the end of the first Bank of the United States, and a failed European wheat crop. The collapse spread eventually even to Giles County, TN. Rush moved the family to Little Rock, on the Western Frontier, around 1845. His daughter Mary Eliza was 17 years old, and Tennessee had left her with a broad definition of elegance and charm.

"I shall never forget the day we arrived. We went to the hotel on the levee. It was the breakfast hour. We took seats at the table, and soon it was filled with guests at every plate, each man laid his Bowie knife or pistol. My father asked his next neighbor what was the matter: was a fight expected? 'Oh no,' he replied, 'everything is quiet.' And you may be assured they were polite."

"General Archibald Yell was the governor (1840–1844) of the state. He came and breakfasted with us, and immediately took us to our home. Elegant people lived here, and life was charming not withstanding much lawlessness."

"Hotel...Water Street above the lower landing, Board with lodging per week $3, single meal 25 cents, keeping horse per day 62 1/2 cents"
Arkansas Banner, February 1845

Arkansas opened very slowly to settlement, hemmed on the east by the Mississippi River and vast wetlands on both shores and on the west by Indian territory.

The original terrain of now seemingly level downtown Little Rock is much changed over time. On the south side of the river, dry land rose somewhat steeply to form the bank from the west, where the bottom land would be the Feild Bros farm, east to the Little Rock where it flattened and allowed for docking boats. The land to the south, i.e., the new town, fell off gradually in the direction of the southern boundary of town. Until after the Civil War, the traveler, soon after leaving town to the south or west, moved through still virgin timber.

It is contemplated to remove the seat of government of the Territory. Land at Little Rock is in the possession of a company of enterprising gentlemen from St. Louis, who have already surveyed and laid off a town; the site of which for natural beauty and advantages is not surpassed by any west of the mountains. It is in unusually elevated situation, for this

country, with a fine service, gradually ascending as you
received from the river for 2 miles, has a rocky beyond
shore with an excellent harbor for boats, being a
semicircular cove free from any current whatever. On the
spot, and in its immediate vicinity is a heavy growth of pine
and cypress timber for building; and what renders it in
valuable as a site for a town, there are several perpetual
springs of good water issuing from the hills—It is more over
the place, and the only place, where a great road from
Missouri to the red river can cross the Arkansas ....
navigable for steamboat to Little Rock during the greater part
of the year. Should the territorial legislature at the ensuing
(October) session pitch upon this place as the seat of
government (and such is unquestionably the wish of the
people) a very few years will make a Little Rock the most
important town in, what is destined to be, one of the most
important states in the American union. (Signed) OSCAR
The *Arkansas Gazette* (Arkansas Post, Arkansas),
Saturday, May 27, 1820

The New Madrid earthquakes (1811–1812) resulted in lands
forever altered, inaccessible, underwater, transformed to swamp or
otherwise untillable. Legislation in 1815 allowed the "materially
injured" a swap for unclaimed land. A speculator Ohara, bought
certificates neighboring the smaller (but first) rock outcropping,
and founded the city of Arkopolis. Unfortunately, the survey
showed the property, in fact, had first belonged to a William Lewis,
then was sold to William Russell. Ohara naturally just moved the
town. He and helpers, who were masked or otherwise had their
identity obscured, used frontier engineering and brute force to drag
buildings west from what would be Scott Street to where Center
Street is today. Chester Ashley claimed to own the new site after
Ohara died. Russell and Ashley went to court. Ultimately lost land
when the Federal Preemption Act of 1830 gave any squatter the

rights to property they had improved. The definition of improvement was often as loose as the character of the claimant.

The 1818 Quapaw Treaty relegated the Tribe to a small territory, marked by the Quapaw Line, a survey running south from La Petit Roche and along the western boundary of the Little Rock Arsenal. In 1819, the Arkansas Territory, including Indian Territory/Oklahoma, was separated from Missouri Territory after a failed effort in Congress to resolve slavery limits. By 1820, Little Rock was a permanent settlement, in the loosest sense. In 1820, Nutall, British explorer, succinctly noted "bachelors" at Little Rock, living together in a "cabin." In context, he flattered neither the men nor the dwelling. Little Rock became the territorial capital, comprising one hotel, one boarding house, and seven private houses. The bachelors and their cabin are all lost in the mists of time, and likely, good riddance to all.

Two keelboats of missionaries headed for Indian territory arrived in 1820 and remained to allow passengers recovery from fevers...

> The arrival of these missionaries was matched to the time and material of our society. There were several well educated and intelligent ladies and gentlemen in the company, who did all they could to render themselves pleasant and useful to us in our secluded and lonely condition. We had divine service every Sabbath and could watch Him work for we were again in a Christian country.

Steamboat travel on the Arkansas River began in 1820, and by 1822 one could travel from Little Rock up the river valley to the Petit Jean River and south as far as Danville, into Yell County. Navigation was, and would be, limited by extremes of current at high water, shallows, snags, and sandbars at low water. When navigable, the twists and turns and switchbacks added many additional miles. Henry Miller Shreve demonstrated a steam-powered snag boat and by 1839 had altered the channel on the Red River. Gradually, this was the game changer for river traffic across the South. In 1840, the two largest towns in Arkansas were to the west, Fort Smith and Van Buren on the Indian Territory border. The centrally located capital Little Rock was third.

Arkansas Native Americans had been pushed and squeezed to Indian Territory in Oklahoma, along with the 7,000 Cherokee, Choctaw, and Chickasaw who passed through town on the Trail of Tears. The wife of Cherokee Chief John Ross, Wlizabet Watie, 34, arrived by riverboat. She arrived weak and ill. She died and was buried in Little Rock.

In 1826 or 1827 Major Isaac Watkins of Little Rock, on what would be later The Farm ("3 miles north of Little Rock"), was shot and killed over two stolen hogs or by a horse thief. Versions of the story vary. By 1855, it was mapped, with two cabins, a well, and the still existing River Road. Scott Street would be named for Andrew Horatio Scott, Superior Court judge of Arkansas Territory. Scott arrived in Arkansas Post as a judge in 1819. In addition to judging, he also managed to kill two men. One was a fellow Superior Court judge. The duel was not over a legal point but rather a lady's honor. The second loser was accused of lying in a local campaign for Territory Delegate. The judge brandished his cane, produced a hidden spear, and killed him. At trial he was acquitted, on a plea of self-defense.

The town and state progressed, albeit at a glacial pace. It was a rough place. "A small cabin made of round logs with the bark on" on what would later be the corner of Fourth and Scott and another "were the only houses then in Little Rock." The "small cabin" may be that of the Dodge home, the purported site of the "Arkansas Traveler" painting by Washburn.

Jesse Hinderliter found a settlement of perhaps 60 buildings, mostly log construction. Around 1827, he opened his log tavern, later covered with clapboards. It is now on the grounds of the Historic Arkansas Museum, preserved as the meeting place of the last Territorial Legislature. In 1833, he confronted two armed assailants, stabbing and killing one. He surrendered to law enforcement immediately, another acquittal as self-defense. A legal strategy was often the argument, "Your Honor, Gentlemen of the Jury, the victim needed a good killin'."

Robert Crittenden, the first lawyer in Little Rock, killed a former friend and later rival, Henry Conway, in a duel. Never punished by the court, he did lose his next election and died later in disgrace, while Conway lingered a week and died, but with his honor intact.

It was 1826 before the denizen citizens of Little Rock would bother to obtain a city charter. The 1820 Missouri Compromise dictated each slave state admitted must be paired with a free state. In 1836 Arkansas petitioned to enter the Union with the free state Michigan, amidst local fears that there might otherwise, be a long wait to pair with another free state, perhaps as long as 25 years. This precipitous move coincided with the start of the devastating Panic of 1837. Whether slave or free, prosperous or subsisting, the granting of statehood ended some supports available to a territory—infrastructure and government operations, especially roads. As a slave state, with only minimal roads and improvements, this would harbinger misplaced priorities and hampered growth and development for a long, long time to come.

The boundary, the Quapaw line, began at La Petite Roche, referred to maybe for the first time in writing as the Little Rock, and south roughly along Rock Street. The tribe, diminished by smallpox,...

called themselves Gappa, by the Americans, Quapaw. A treaty in 1824 yielded their lands...to our government for certain considerations... "1826 consisting of 158 men, 123 women emigrated under the conduct of an Indian Agent." The Letters of Governor George Izard to the American Philosophical Society 1825–1827

Two blocks west of the line, in 1837 Col William Gilchrist built a west facing house on the 800 block Scott Street, though not without injury. Gilchrest was a Master of the Masonic Lodge, but less so a carpenter.

> On Tuesday last, Colonel William Gilchrist and Mr. J. Ringstaff as Carpenter were on the shingling scaffold of Mr. Gilchrist's house when the scaffold gave way and Mr. Gilchrist was precipitated to the ground, two stories and in the fall broke his left arm and was otherwise badly bruised. Mr. Ringstaff escaped unhurt by catching hold of the shingling, and afterwards descended the side of the house.
> *Weekly Arkansas Gazette*, 1837

In 1842, Will's brother, Silas, built on the southwest corner of what is now Ninth and Cumberland. According to different family members over the generations, there are three different years of Rush and family's arrival. These are 1842, 1843, and 1845. All are anecdotal. The 1845 Scott property would have been laid out in a similar layout.

Construction of a town began, 1836 a State Capitol; 1840 Little Rock Arsenal established by U.S. Army; 1840–1842, construction of Episcopal Church at Fifth and Scott. In 1844, Gilchrist died "suddenly," and Rush and family moved to 811. In 1845 Rush was selected Judge of the State Fifth Circuit by the Legislature. Rush was a last-minute 1846 Candidate for State Senate against Thomas Newton, filing 10 days before the election. The same Newton fought a duel in 1827 that, in part, had origins in the squabble over the property that had become Little Rock. No one was injured, and the affair was considered closed with honor (sic). Rush's last-minute surprise upset William (Billy) Woodruff, founder of the *Arkansas Gazette*, enough to denounce him with a potential fighting allegation, "disorganizer."

DENOUNCED A MAN WHOSE DEMOCRACY HAS NEVER
BEEN QUESTIONED HERE OR ELSEWHERE, AS A
DISORGANIZER, FOR PERMITTING HIS NAME TO BE
USED, AT THE CALL OF HIS POLITICAL FRIENDS, AS A
CANDIDATE FOR THE SENATE AGAINST A WHIG!! And
why this denunciation? Colonel TW Newton, an
uncompromising Whig, ... Hence the view of Billy
Woodruff, it was disorganization in the Democratic Party to
call upon one of their party.
Arkansas Gazette, Little Rock, October 2, 1847

Provocation was a serious, and often deadly business. When the votes were counted, Newton prevailed. He was an opponent of the dominant political faction, The Family, AKA the Sevier-Crittenden Faction. The Family controlled early state government. Through blood and marriage and insider knowledge, they controlled the Federal survey of massive wilderness acreage, which provided benefits for themselves and cronies. Newton fought a duel in the 1830s with Ambrose Sevier over a slight to then-Governor Crittenden. Both men fired guns, but neither was hit, and their seconds, with cooler heads, prevailed.

William Woodruff played the role of disorganizer in the extreme. John Garret, a deputy sheriff, visited Woodruff's office seeking Chester Ashley, for the purpose of "cowhiding" Ashley. Garret returned, but this time Ashley and Woodruff were both there. Four shots were fired; Garret was dead of gunshot wounds. A three-day coroner's inquest referred no charges

"Unable to determine from any evidence before the court to
ascertain by whom the mortal wound was given"

Governor Yell, who greeted fellow Tennesseans, Rush et al, at the heavily armed breakfast table the day they arrived in

Little Rock, was himself involved in dueling. He left Tennessee over blowback from a duel with yet another newspaper editor. Amidst all the violence and killing, the Feild-Newton election ended with only ink spilled.

The City advertised to bridge the meandering Town Branch at the north end of Scott Street at Cherry Street (Second). The low bid bridge washed away soon. After, little would be done until the Union occupation. Flooding, stench, and filth were not resolved until it was finally covered in 1928. It still flows, but unseen and odor free, beneath the streets of the City today.

Gold was discovered in California, overnight shifting the horizon of the Frontier 2,000 miles to the Pacific Coast. Arkansas borders remained hemmed by geography to the east and to the west by Indian territory. That same year, Rush's election campaign letter appeared alongside the advertised sale of another human being.

To the voters of the Fifth Judicial Circuit.

Since the light amendment to the constitution of the state, the governor has made proclamation that an election will be held on the first Monday of February next, for a Circuit judge of this district. Should it be the wish of the people to continue me in the office, which I've held for the last two years by an election of the legislature, I will thankfully receive such approbation and assurance by your votes on the day of election specified in the proclamation. Having presided in all the counties of this new circuit, except Conway, Pope, and Yell, I suppose my character in standing is known to the greater part of this constituency the voters of the new counties I refer to the profession who are acquainted with me. Should I receive your suffrage I promise a faithful discharge of duty.
Your fellow citizen,
William H Feild
Little Rock, January 23, 1849

AUCTION
Will be sold on SATURDAY the 27th inst. at 2 o'clock pm at
OFFICERS CORNER a likely NEGRO BOY about 20 years
old. For particulars apply to JAS D FITZGERALD, Auctioneer
Arkansas Gazette, January 1849

The country was changing around Arkansas, but King Cotton swaggered along, and chattel slavery was staggering beside it.

The South without the North would continue in her onward
March, prosperity yearly increasing in numbers, wealth, and
power... if either party has a cause of alarm, it is the North
that ought to dread a rupture with the South.
Weekly Arkansas Gazette, 24 May 1850, Page 4

Or maybe not. The 1850 Census Little Rock population was 2,167. Scott Street neighbors were now mostly Arkansas born, and all were U.S. native born. In his mid 20s on arrival in the state, Will began in mercantile in Little Rock, probably with Uncle Silas. He moved to Yell County and continued in business there. After two years merchanting, he detoured to read law, was examined before a judge and local attorney, and admitted to the bar.

After being engaged in the practice of law for 2 years at
Danville, he decided there were some phases of the law that
did not measure up to the distinct principles of honesty to
which he adhered, and he accordingly abandoned his
profession and returned to mercantile pursuits.
Hempstead 1911, vol 2

The Kentucky-born Presley Jameson family settled in Johnson County by 1838 and farmed Arkansas River bottom land. The1850 U.S. Census recorded Will and his new business partner, Sam Dolley, as merchants living with the Jameson household in Spring

Creek, not much more than a stone's throw from Danville. Adjoining neighbors' places of birth reflected those of the frontier, originating from all over—Arkansas, Tennessee, Alabama, Scotland, Ireland, and Germany. Yell County split from Johnson, had 3,300 residents, about three persons per square mile. Yell County was not in the Delta, but Jameson enslaved 13, only two of which were adults. Their neighbor and in-law in Spring Creek Township, John Howell, enslaved more people than any other county resident. In 1852, Will married the farmer's daughter, Mary Rebecca (1834–1909). Unlike his father's betrothed, his bride was a respectable 20 years old. The Bros followed, WP in 1854, Ernest in 1857, and Joe was born in Danville in 1859.

In the 1850 U.S. Census Slave Schedule, Will and Sam were listed with one enslaved person in Pulaski County while their primary residence was in Yell County. Rush's neighbor Dr William Cantrell at 619 Scott saw the patients at the County indigent hospital, i.e., white indigents, as well as at a practice from his home. No slackers were allowed among the poor and ill.

[T]hose capable of working will be required to take such gentle exercise as will improve their health and assist to earn their bread
Arkansas Banner, November 1851

In 1851, Rush, after selection by General Assembly, won in the first popular vote for circuit judge. This campaign was better organized than his disorganized Senate campaign and carried all six counties in the Fifth Circuit, with 1,408 votes to 800. Thomas Newton, dueling days behind him, sat with Rush in peace on the board of the Little Rock High School for Young Ladies.

Little Rock High School
Under the care of Mrs. and the Misses Woods Business will be resumed 1 of September when a punctual attendance of

the pupils is respectfully requested. The board of visitors to the above institution well satisfied from long personal observation, that its accomplished proprietors are highly competent to teach, in the most approved and successful manner, all the branches of a thorough and finished education, therefore take great pleasure in recommending to a continuation of that large and increasing patronage which it has enjoyed since commencement.

August 22, 1851

The local luminaries on the 14-member Board of Visitors were four attorneys, a minister, a general, a major, a captain, and a physician. Not one female strained their pretty little heads in guiding the school. In 1853, the city opened a public school, of sorts, at Seventh and Scott. With 9,000 miles of track in operation in the North, the Little Rock–Fort Smith Railroad incorporated. But, in no hurry for progress or connection to a larger world, no track would be laid for a decade.

The U.S. Army Little Rock Arsenal was around the corner from 811, at Ninth and Rock. By this time, any threat from Native Americans, if indeed one had ever existed, was imaginary. By the time the Bros were old enough to leave the grounds of 811, out the back gate, and see the 36-acre grounds ahead, it would have been a two-minute walk, or a one-minute boy gallop, east past Rock Street. The Arsenal was impressive with a main Tower Building and multiple outbuildings. The marching soldiers, firearms, bands, shouting, bugling and drumming, and marching would have been a magnet for boys. When WP and Ernest were small, a local matron described big doings round the corner, The Arsenal in the whirl of local society.

I am very busy at this time helping the girls fix for a May party they are going to have on Tuesday. They will have a

coronation at 5 o'clock at the Arsenal—the loveliest spot I most
ever saw—& at night they will have their party which they have
gotten up by contribution at the school building. Mr. [Albert]
Pike's eldest daughter—Isadore—is to be Queen of May.
1856: Margaret Sarah (Breckinridge) Johnson letter to
Marguerite A. C. Menzies

The 1836 Constitution provided for two state banks, the Real
Estate Bank for land and the State Bank for agriculture and consumer
banking. The Panic of 1837 that relocated the family in Arkansas,
clobbered speculative frontier finances. By 1843, the Bank stopped
operations. The bonds issued, debts, leadership or lack thereof, and
subsequent trusteeship were worthy of farce, but real to citizens. One
knifing and death on the floor of the legislature, and another broken
up, before bloodshed, are part of the sordid history. The court case
over disposition of the bonds, the debt, the entire mess, landed in
Rush's Fifth Circuit Court. The slow pace of the docket, including
illness of the court clerk, and political machinations of the whole
fiasco led to legislation, supported by the governor. The case involved
the Trustees of the Bank, one of whom was the clerk in question. The
business establishment, political and legal, finally decided, enough.
The new law established a first, separate Chancery Court, which
immediately assumed jurisdiction for the case.

Fifth of January 1855
To The President Of The Senate Of The General Assembly
Of The State Of Arkansas:
For the office of chancellor under the act entitled "An act to
establish a separate court of Chancery at the seat of
government, so that the causes of the state, including that
against the trustees and officers of the Real Estate Bank, and
those of individuals, may be determined as early as
practicable...."
Elias N Conway

With the dubious honor of inspiring an entirely new court system, Rush resigned the same day, in a spirit of "You can't fire me, I quit."

"Hon. Wm. H. Feild has resigned the office of Judge of this Judicial Circuit"
Arkansas State Gazette and Democrat, January 1855

William H Feild, late judge of the Fifth Judicial Circuit, will attend to business entrusted to him in the several Courts here, and in the river country below this place,
February 7, 1855
Arkansas True Democrat, October 1

There was no judicial greatness in Rush's handling of the case. But taking it away and a new court did nothing to solve the problems. The last stake was finally driven through the Bank's heart in 1898. Part of the fallout was reflected in the First Amendment to the Arkansas Constitution, which in 1846 outlawed banks. In a young farming state needing capital to grow, Arkansas voters outlawed banks.

Party politics were complex. In Pine Bluff, Isaac Mills, whose great-granddaughter would marry Pappaw, had been active in the American Party, anti-immigrant, anti-Catholic, known as Know Nothing Party. The Party was divided on slavery, but in Arkansas, it was pro Union. Isaac stood as a candidate in 1852 for state representative. In 1855, he was one of the multiples of State Party vice presidents, who …

resolved, that utterly forgetting all former political creeds and differences, we will henceforth have but one flag, and that the good old American flag.
THE PRESERVATION AND PERPETUATION OF THE UNION OF THE STATES, NOW AND FOREVER!"
Arkansas Gazette, August 1856

Will, Silas, and Sam Dolley were in the mercantile trade as Feild and Dolley in both Little Rock and Danville in Yell County. They divided the enterprise, with Will in Danville near the in-laws and starting a family. In 1859, Will shifted to Little Rock, but not before he was named Postmaster of Danville, a patronage position. The political sinecure was from President Buchanan, supporter of the pro-slavery Dred Scott decision and of admission of Bloody Kansas as a slave state. Their convoluted arrangements of being two places at once were explained below, Silas going one way, Sam and Will the other.

DISSOLUTION NOTICE
The partnership of the undersigned in the Mercantile houses in Little Rock and Danville in this state is by agreement dissolved, in the following manner: William H Feild of said firm withdraws from the house at Little Rock and surrenders all his interest in the same, from the commencement thereof to Silas F Feild and Samuel F Dolley, they paying all debts and liabilities incurred for and on account of said house. And the said Silas F Feild and Samuel F Dolley hereby withdraw and surrender all their interest in the house at Danville, from the commencement of the same to William H. Feild of Danville, he to receive all the proceeds from the same and pay all its debts in debts and liabilities. The name of the company is only retained by the parties to close the unsettled business of the firm.
Wm H Feild
Sam'l F Dolley
Silas F Feild
Little Rock, June 25, 1855

Advertising tells the story of the firm and local business.

The True Democrat, July 1855
Messrs. Feild, Dolley & Co, having received a large portion
of their stock, desire to exchange it for money as soon as
possible. As the liberal dealer is ever known by the amount of
advertising which he does, it is reasonable to suppose that
this farm will attach themselves a large custom. See adv'ts.

"Feild, Dolly (sic) and Co
Dealers in foreign and domestic dry goods, pants, boots,
shoes, hardware, groceries, et cetera at the store family
occupied by S Joseph, Main Street, have on hand, and are
now receiving a large and general assortment of
merchandise in their line which they are selling at prices
desirable to purchasers. They ask that person to purchasing
should call and examine their stock.
Little Rock, June 9, 1854

Notice! Notice!
All persons indebted to the undersigned by note or account
are requested to come forward at once, if possible, and pay
up. We are at this time in great need of money to pay our own
debts and are bound to make collections in order to do so.
Feild and Dolley
Arkansas Gazette, January 1860

VI.
GODLY CHRISTIANS SECEDE

And the Lord said—What hast thou done? The voice of thy
brother's blood crieth unto me from the ground.
Genesis 4:10

Freedom is unquestionably the birth right of all mankind;
Africans as well as Europeans: to keep the former in a state
of slavery is a constant violation of that right, and therefore
also of justice.
Thoughts Upon Slavery,
John Wesley, 1774

Along with Baptists and Presbyterians, Methodists accommodated what Wesley abhorred. Wesley's words connect to 811, so this focus is on Methodism. Wesley witnessed slavery while in the Colony of Georgia 1736–37. Ten full years before American Methodism separated from Anglicans, his 1774 treatise, *Thoughts On Slavery*, recorded in detail the evils of slavery, the horrors of transport from Africa to middle passage transport, to laboring, living, and dying in American colonies. Methodism in the United States evolved and then, after Wesley's death, separated from the British origins as the Methodist Episcopal Church in 1784. In the

South the churches exchanged the evil Wesley described, acting both on enslaver and enslaved and his support of abolition, for the enslavers' benign obligation to educate the enslaved. In Little Rock, the Feild Bros congregation is now First United Methodist Church Little Rock, or to family, simply First Church.

Rev. Andrew Hunter, known to family then and now as Grandpa Hunter (1813–1902), has been called the Father of Arkansas Methodism. He was to be WP's father-in law, born in County Antrim Ireland, and immigrated with his family to Pennsylvania very young. He was made of stern stuff, and the job required it.

> I was teaching school in ...(near)... St. Louis ... asking God to direct me in my life-work. I did not know whether I was called to preach or not, but I did feel a desire to be (the) call for teachers for the Indian schools reached me, I felt I could enter that field, and if I could not preach I could at least teach ... when the opening was presented.... my journey of 300 and more miles.... (From) Fayetteville, I started alone into the Indian country ... in search of the Superintendent of Indian Missions. Pleasant Berryhill lived on the south bank of the Verdigris; he was a half-breed (sic) and a Methodist, and from him I obtained information ...The next morning, I found my man ...(who)... received me as a messenger sent in answer to prayer. ... south of the Arkansas (River), in the Creek Nation (Indian Territory, later Oklahoma), to teach school equipped with blankets, a buffalo robe and a new bed-tick, which was to be filled with new cut hay chopped up fine with an axe.... Few days in town, I started across the Arkansas River, and in school master at Hichity Town ...(near present day Muskogee) ... was inaugurated monarch of all I surveyed. I would like to know what became of my pupils there, doubtless some of them are citizens of the Creek Nation. How happy I would be if I knew that anything said or done by me had influenced any life for the better. There in

that little log schoolhouse I preached my first sermon. It was through an interpreter; twenty or thirty persons were present and heard my discourse on the conversion of Cornelius, the Roman centurion."

Grandpa Hunter was named pastor of First Methodist Episcopal, known locally then as the Cherry Street (now Second Street) Methodist, then as "First Church" 1841, 1844–45, ministering to 66 whites and 141 "colored."

In 1836, the national meeting of the Methodist Episcopal Church recorded…

"where is great excitement has prevailed in this country, on the subject of modern abolitionism, etc., Resolved by the delegates of the Annual Conference, in General Conference, assembled that they are decidedly opposed to modern abolitionism, and holy disclaim, any right, wish, or intention to interfere in the civil and political relations between master and slave, as it exists in the slave holding states."

Grandpa Hunter was one of three delegates from this slave holding state to the 1848 ME General Conference. A proxy for the long simmering question of enslavement loomed. The subject, a bishop, who did, or did not own slaves, that were, or were not inherited, were or were not his wife's, or had been freed, but preferred enslavement. The three voted the party line, that in slaveholding states, local laws allowing enslavement trumped any and all moral, biblical, and denominational authority. The next year, the final document left no question as to the division

"Be resolved that the delegates of the several annual conferences of the Methodist Episcopal Church in the slaveholding states, in general convention, assembled, that it is right, expedient, and necessary to erect the annual

conferences ...separate from the jurisdiction ... of the
Methodist Episcopal Church."

The country now had the Methodist, Episcopal Church, and the officially renamed Methodist Episcopal Church–South

Grandpa Hunter was locally credited as participating in brokering the split.

"How happy I would be if I knew that anything said or done by me had influenced any life for the better."

Will joined the Methodist Episcopal–South Church around 1850.

White congregants numbered 150, and 296 enslaved, and the Church outgrew the space available in 1853. The enslaved were relocated to a site, now Wesley Chapel. It was two blocks from 811, near Mt Holly Cemetery, and was governed by Cherry Street Board. From 1854, it was led by William Wallace Andrews, enslaved by Chester Ashley. After the Federals arrived, he became pastor, and the congregation voted to align with ME–North, in the Missouri Conference. Wesley Chapel opened the first school for freedmen, and in 1867 Walden Seminary, later to become Philander Smith College, organized with classes taught in the church.

Grandpa Hunter was twice pastor at First Church, in 1842 and 1866–67. He was elected to the Arkansas Senate, then as President of Senate. In January 1867, a delegation from the legislature was sent to Washington, D.C., opposing suffrage for African Americans. Grandpa Hunter led the group, meeting with President Andrew Johnson—twice. The President was in agreement.

Grandpa was elected by the General Assembly for U.S. Senate in December 1866, but never seated.

My election was most unexpected by me.... After mature
deliberation I find I cannot accept the honor conferred
without injury to the church of which I am a minister.
Arkansas Gazette, February 1867

Grandpa Hunter was certainly not an abolitionist, or Unionist; conducting a burial, or comforting the sick and wounded would have been sufficient to bar him being seated.

The War cooled religious zeal. the Little Rock Church reported 185 white members in 1861, and the next report available, 1866, 132 white members. During the Occupation, the Methodist Episcopal Church, i.e., anti-slavery, or Northern, or original Church, placed a pastor in the pulpit on property of the local church "sustained by the military" WP and Ernest should have attended Confirmation Classes during this time, until President Johnson commanded the "return of the house to its rightful owners," the ME–South.

A larger edifice was needed. Little Rock First Methodist Episcopal Church South (ME-S), completed in 1878, destroyed by fire in 1895. On a bitter cold day, the custodian had overloaded the furnace with more fuel than usual, which proved to be too much. Two firefighters lost their lives. WP was chiseled on the marble dedication plaque for the rebuilt sanctuary in 1898, and in 1918, served on the building committee for a new Chapel.

The Bros were to be on best behaviors, as WP was Sunday School Superintendent for many years. A photo from First Church, 1919, shows WP, Pappaw, and Presley on the front steps of the Church, members of the all-male Board of Stewards.

In the 1960s, my family was told that a portrait of Andrew Hunter had been discovered in the church basement, and Daddy was invited to the unveiling. Seeing a handsome portrait of a handsome older gentleman, 19th century, Daddy knew it was not Grandpa Hunter. Hence the actual photo was found and is now in the History Hall exhibit of photos at First Church. His stern, imposing face reflects an early life of buffalo skins, sleeping on the ground, and an intimate familiarity with an axe.

The groups un-schismed in 1939. The reunited Church divided by geography into regional Conferences—except African American pastors and congregations, who all comprised a Central Jurisdiction made up out of whole cloth. In 1969, when Methodists and United Brethren denominations merged into the United Methodist Church, the Central jurisdiction ceased to exist, and geography instead of skin pigment determined affiliation. Eleven years after the integration of Little Rock Central High School, Uncle Joe's legacy, Methodist-affiliated Hendrix College, integrated in 1965.

Hunter Memorial Methodist Church was built in 1897 and dedicated by Grandpa in 1901. The congregation later moved to Romine Road in Little Rock and is now a vibrant African American ministry. The photo of his stern visage in old age, who negotiated a denomination schism and lobbied President Grant against suffrage for freedmen, hangs in the foyer of the sanctuary.

VII.
BEING THE WEAKEST OF
THE "COTTON CONFEDERACY"

(Arkansas) would then be the only considerable cotton
growing state in the Union .... She (Arkansas) is to choose
between being the weakest of the "Cotton Confederacy" and
without hope of ever being stronger, exposed to all the
horrors of border warfare, and occupying the highest
position of any state in the union with a general government
armed with the power and charged with the duty of guarding
and protecting her
Arkansas Gazette, February 2, 1861

The above words are among the saddest of the many sad ones
written. In Pulaski County, Joseph Stillwell and Augustus Garland
took out ads together and stood as anti-secession candidates.
Stillwell published a lengthy letter, excerpted above. While in no
way supporting abolition, or emancipation, he made a strong case
for staying with loyal border states.

A brief letter published on the same page from Augustus Garland
announced his own candidacy and endorsed Stillwell's sentiments
above. Their sound arguments were true, but not compelling.

"Weakest in the Cotton Confederacy"
"no hope of ever being stronger"

Arkansas was a distant fifth in the nation for cotton production. The Dred Scott decision in 1857 ruled no Negro or descendant of slaves was a citizen of the U.S. The emboldened governor and general assembly quickly adopted

"An Act to Remove the Free Negroes and Mulattoes
from this State,"
1859 Act No. 151.

No state had fewer than Arkansas's 700 free Negroes, but it was now illegal to draw breath as a free African American anywhere in the state, according to the *Arkansas Gazette*, January 1860.

The enslaved population in Arkansas ranked 11th out of the 15 slave states. These were not randomly or widely distributed. Of almost 60,000 households, only 1,149 had enslaved persons. Of those, 490 reported more than five enslaved persons. In the 1850 and 1860 U.S. Census, a Schedule 2 was added entitled Slave Schedule.

Entries included "Name of Slave Owner" and individuals identified by age, gender, and color, "black" or "mulatto." Rush was listed as "Name of Slave Owner," 19 individuals.

Slave inhabitants on the City of Little Rock in the County of
Pulaski of Arkansas, enumerated by me on the eighth day of
June 1860—GW Simpson
WH Field

The entry of WH Feild was, Males ages 30, 6, 14, 1, 35, 18, 16 and females ages 22, 22, 6½, 3, 10, 8, 4, 1, 18, 18. County tax records listed 14 people, from one-year-old boy and girl to a 35-year-old man. On the same Census record page are his brother

Silas listing "1, 13 F" and William Woodruff of the *Gazette*, 11, ranging from a "70, M to a 2, M." Rush's Will when probated included, by the laws of the day, "goods and chattels, rights and credit" "full power to secure and dispose of said property," which included all the people above.

In modern parlance, the practice and wide acceptance of chattel slavery—the enslavement of four million men, women, and children—had become too big to fail. Over the history of the nation, 1,800 members of Congress enslaved other humans. Various guesstimates of the economics of enslaving humans included seven times the value of circulating U.S. currency, 12 times the value of King Cotton, or more than the valuation of all manufacturing and railroads combined.[1] Labor markets north and south, opportunities for small farmers, artisans, and craftsmen were distorted by the presence of enslavers and the enslaved, from 811 and across the ocean. Northern insurance companies insured the enslaved as property, and ocean fleets transported the cotton cultivated and picked by enslaved. In the UK textile mills, the associated capital and labor markets awaited those bales arriving. Other ships returned with the imports financed by cotton.

It would require the payor of last resort to lay out the blood and treasure to finally end it.

In 1860 WP was six, Ernest three, Joe one. Lincoln did not campaign as an abolitionist, but as opposed to incessant efforts to extend chattel slavery not just to the rest of the country, but south as far as Central America and offshore to Cuba. He opposed the Fugitive Slave Act and chattel slavery in the Federal jurisdiction, Washington City/ District of Columbia. And for the Union.

---

[1] See *Carry Me Back: The Domestic Slave Trade in American Life* by Steven Deyle (Oxford University Press, 2006) and *How the Word Is Passed: A Reckoning with the History of Slavery Across America* by Clint Smith (Little, Brown and Company, 2022).

We call upon every man be he Whig, American, or
Democrat and eschewing partisanship cast his vote for Bell
Everett and the Union.
Weekly Arkansas Gazette, 20 October 1860

Lincoln was not even on ballots in Arkansas. Had he been, and suffrage been universal, the outcome would have perhaps been different, looking at the 1860 Census: population of LR 3,727, 325 enslavers, 846 enslaved. John Breckinridge, the sitting U.S. Vice President, won the state handily, went on to serve in the Confederate Army. In time to report nominating conventions, elections, and events that followed, the telegraph line arrived in town. Arkansas, under pressure from both enslavers and Unionists, set the Secession Convention for March 4, 1861.

Lincoln took office March 4, 1861. In a State with two percent of households with enslaved person, 40 percent of Convention delegates were slaveholders. In a passing moment of reality and good sense, the Convention voted down Secession 40–35. Stillwell and Garland having been duly elected duly cast their NO votes. In cart-before-the-horse fashion, on threat of violence, U.S. troops had already been withdrawn from the Arsenal on February 8, 1861. In a town of 4,000, six so-called militia units of 1,000 men gathered, with a threat to raise 5,000. Although denying he was responsible, Governor Rector demanded the commander, Captain Totten, surrender the Arsenal.

"... in the present emergency the arms and munitions of war in the Arsenal should be under the control of the State authorities, ... This movement, although not authorized by me, ... it becomes my duty, ... to prevent a collision between the people of the State and the Federal troops under your command. I therefore demand...possession of the Arsenal and munitions ....to the State authorities, to be held subject to the action of the (scheduled Secession) Convention..."

In a spirit of "hail fellow well met, and even better gone," the self-described ladies of Little Rock, i.e., white women, presented the U.S. Commander an engraved sword on his way out of the town.

At the Second Convention, delegates including Garland and Stillwell, now either swept along, or with cynical resignation, duly cast YES votes to secede, leaving only Isaac Murphy the sole NO vote. Rush died on May 10, 1861, four days afterward. Arkansas was, as predicted, the weakest in the Cotton Confederacy, with no hope of ever being stronger. With a state capital population of 3,600 and statewide, in distant last place among all states, 38 miles of railroad, Arkansas went to war. The following year, Lincoln would sign the Transcontinental Rail Act. War or no, May 4, Yankee sweets and liquor were for sale, and three weeks later, on May 25, Feild and Dolley offered 150 Gallons of Ohio Whiskey for sale.

Candy
25 boxes of candy, received and for sale by
Feild and Dolley
January 12, 1861
Whiskey
30 bbls. Old Reserve Whiskey
Five 10 gal. kegs Old Bourbon
Five 10 gal. kegs Old Rye
Five 10 gal. kegs Old Monongahela Whiskey
January 12,1861, Feild & Dolley

Both advertisements began in January and continued to run weekly through May, for the sweet tooth and thirst.

The 1861 Pulaski County Tax Assessment lists 325 individuals holding enslaved persons, and the valuation of human lives. Humans enslaved, enslavers taxed, revenue collected, local, state, and federal governments kept the accounts.

Accounting standards varied by jurisdiction. Some records did not record enslaved persons younger than five or older than 60.

The town, such as it was, basically ceased to function. The public school closed, and not for the last time. City council meetings ceased soon after. The War started Wednesday, May 29, 1861.

We arrived at Little Rock about 3 o'clock P.M. but was until 5 o'clock getting across the Arkansas River. When we got on the West bank we proceeded up street & halted, after some delay a band was brought forth & we were cordially welcomed (with banners flying in the breeze) to the city and were escorted with music to the College ground 1 mile south of the city where we took Quarters for the present.
T. Jeff Job, CSA, diary, May 25–August 6, 1861

A short lived welcome, as soldiers and civilians already began to sour on one another by 1862. Deserters, grifters, prostitutes, and the usual camp followers congregated around dwindling supplies, and morale. Trans Mississippi Commander General Hindman was concerned enough to establish a Little Rock Provost Guard to keep order. Locally known as Willets Guard, it was commanded by a Mr. Willet, a blacksmith and Freemason, and three lieutenants, including a head waiter at the Fril-Fral Hotel for Gentlemen, and a livery stable operator. A Confederate soldier's letter home said of Little Rock,

"The rich set back and seem to regard the wet and hungry soldier as something beneath their notice."

July 4, 1863, brought Union victories of the siege of Vicksburg, the Battle of Gettysburg, and the fall of Helena Arkansas. The entire length of the Mississippi River was open, and the Union advance to Little Rock began. The loss of Little Rock was inevitable, and Lincoln appointed a military governor for Arkansas, hoping for early reconstruction. Conditions had further deteriorated in town.

"the secretary of war hereby recognizes impressment as a legal and operative mode of securing necessary supplies of sustenance, medical, and quartermaster stores.... The quartermaster general, commissary general, and surgeon general may designate the officer and persons ... to make impressment to accumulate supplies ... No officer or agent shall impress the necessary supplies which any person may have for the consumption of himself, his family, employees, slaves..."
Congress CSA, April 1862

"To provide for the relief of needy and destitute families of soldiers in this State, and began to collect "name of soldier, county, where enlisted, regiment, where serving, active duty, dead, or discharged, names of family members, and ages, and relationship to soldier"
Arkansas General Assembly, Dec 1, 1862.

State government fled to Hot Springs in May 1863, only to return two weeks later. By June 1863, another contemporary seemed to blame the town.

"Our Army was greatly contaminated by our stay in Little Rock, particularly the Officers giving themselves to licentiousness and drunkenness."

By the end of the war, persons who had been enslaved property were free, and the currency was worthless, and the state remained, as predicted, "the weakest of the 'Cotton Confederacy'" with no "hope of ever being stronger."

> "I was the partner of Mr. Dolley at the time that picture was taken, and you will see our firm naming Feild & Dolley over the door of the building now standing on the site of the present Exchange National Bank. Mr. Dolley died in this city after the war. We operated the business in ...1859, 1860, and 1861, moving across the street.... During the war I had a lot of meat on hand which was taken, ... he gave me a receipt for it, and so much Confederate money that I never took time to count it."
> Little Rock,1903 Board of Trade publication)

Enslaved people were restive as the Federals approached, and Confederate soldiers were sullen, as the Union forces moved up from Helena. General Steele deemed necessary General Order 5, Part VI, issued August 12, 1863, at the start of the approach to Little Rock.

> No property shall be taken from citizens without authority.... Straggling, marauding, and setting buildings on fire are positively forbidden. Any infraction will be summarily punished, and any officer who shall fail to notice such infraction shall be deemed guilty of neglect of duty.... These measures are necessary for the sake of discipline, and as a matter of policy towards the people of Arkansas, whom we desire to bring back to their allegiance...

The last week of August 1863, Will was paid off as a civilian CSA purchasing agent. The *Weekly Gazette*, espousing a mix of fatalism and optimistic life as usual, noted Confederate General

Kirby Smith speculated permanent occupation of Little Rock would be delayed until winter. The *Arkansas State Gazette* noted a Federal withdrawal to Clarendon indicated no plans for an imminent invasion. St. Mary's Academy for Girls was enrolling for a regular fall term, $175 tuition and board.

F. Carpenter advertised...

> $200 for the return of (enslaved) Nancy ... near her confinement and her legs considerably swollen (and 3 children, ages 10, 8, and 5).
> *Arkansas Gazette*, August 22 and 29, 1863

But the news also advertised for donations to the local Medical Corps, "'destitute' of bandages." Confederate officials ordered all able-bodied troops switched to Infantry and called for civilians to take up the slack. Strips may have been torn from the ladies' petticoats, but from there zeal dwindled rapidly.

Across the river, seven miles east, Union troops skirmished and Confederates fell back. Walker, the Confederate cavalry commander, challenged his second in command, Marmaduke, to a duel over performance during the Battle of Helena. On September 5, they and their seconds met near Bayou Meto, with pistols, at 15 paces. They met, fired, and both missed. On a second round, Walker was shot dead—over a battle already fought and lost, and on the eve of another, with the same outcome, a fitting coda. General Steele ordered Marmaduke removed and arrested, then, with no leader for his horse soldiers, countermanded his own orders. General Smith's advice had been to put up defense as best could be mounted and to burn cotton stores. The city would depend on "those remaining and less reliable (troops)" rather than the hoped for, but never arrived "best and spirited." The river defenses lacked an ironclad gunboat, but the one tin-clad, CSS *Pontchartrain*, was scuttled near the north shore without firing a shot. It remains on the river bottom; the exact location is not public to prevent disturbing the wreck. The governor called for men to rally to Little Rock, but to little effect. The call to burn one's own cotton was widely ignored.

On September 10, 1863, Federal troops returned to Little Rock for the first time since they left the Arsenal in 1861. Referred to as the occupation of Little Rock, it was liberation for the enslaved. The Bros, now ages nine, six, and three, were witnesses of Confederate and Federal live fire of artillery and rifles, the fading Rebel Yells, Northern accents with likely some Irish and German voices as well. Well-fed, well-equipped, and well-armed Federals marched past Scott Street and turned to the undefended Arsenal, intact with powder, cartridges and five cannons, as the last CSA left Little Rock that afternoon. Considering the capture of a state capital was the result, casualty deaths were light, 137 Federal, Confederate 37. After occupation, the Arsenal compound was a military hospital, with 8,000 treated in 1865. The battle left Little Rock essentially unscathed. Steele's army moved south, leaving an occupation force in place.

VIII.

OCCUPATION, LIBERATION, RECONSTRUCTION

All persons born or naturalized in the United States, and
subject to the jurisdiction thereof, are citizens of the United
States and of the state wherein they reside. No state ... shall
abridge the privileges or immunities of citizens ...; nor ...
deprive any person of life, liberty, or property, without due
process of law; nor ... equal protection of the laws.
14th Amendment, 1868

The right of citizens of the United States to vote shall not be
denied or abridged ... on account of race, color, or
previous condition of servitude.
Section 1, 15th Amendment, 1870

The State government decamped a second and final time to
Washington, Arkansas, taking reality with it, down the rabbit hole
of irony-free delusions. Reporting that Steele approached with
11,000 Federals, men in Little Rock, even those in their 60s, were
in the trenches, the news reporting repeatedly failing the irony test:

It were almost worth the cost to have the enemy invade every
county in the state that our citizens be aroused.
Washington Telegraph, September 9, 1863

We feel sure when the whole matter comes to be
investigated it will be found that Gen Price acted with
judgement and gallantry.... for the protection of South
Arkansas... and the good of the Department, to have lost it
(i.e., his 1,200 Confederates) would have lost the whole of
our state at a blow."
Washington Telegraph, September 16, 1863

The loss of LR has been expected and is really a matter of
little importance as affecting the cause of the South. There is
no occasion for depression, but much to rouse us to energy.
Washington Telegraph, September 16, 1863

Two thousand retreating Confederates had their irony functioning, for the whole affair. Deserting toward their homes or join-
ing in guerilla rabbles, fighting against anyone who got in the way
of pillage, be they Unionist, Confederate, or by this time, the
largest faction of 'leave us alone."

The Federal Headquarters at Markham and Scott streets was in
Chester Ashley's large home. Between there and 811, Federal Commander General Steele took the Albert Pike home on Rock Street.

Major Henry P. Spellman, Seventh Missouri Cavalry, and his
staff soon moved into 811.

The spacious home with its large rooms and comfortable and
attractive appointments proved admirably suited to the
demands of the Federal forces, and they were careful in
preserving order and neatness and in disturbing as little as
possible the domestic affairs of the family. The old
homestead is located at 811 Scott and may be considered

one of the landmarks of the capital city. At the time of the war, the Feild homestead was on the outskirts of the small village of LR and was in the middle of large and well-kept grounds comprising now a city block."
Historical Review of Arkansas: Its Commerce, Industry and Modern Affairs, Volume 2, Fay Hempstead, 1911

No member of Spellman's Seventh was killed, captured, wounded, or missing during the battle. That perhaps led to more benevolent relations, with the family allowed to remain in part of the home, and the family and the building were seemingly well treated. Two blocks over, at Rock and Cumberland, 14-year-old Yvon (sic, pronounced Ivan?) Pike, son of Albert Pike, wrote of memories of the Occupation in a 1926 letter.

"I remained in Little Rock for about a year, in that house, and knew General Steele and most of his staff very well, as he took possession of the house except a small portion occupied by us. They also took possession of the schoolhouse in the yard, for subordinates. This was about a month or so after the surrender. They were not used by the Federals before this time. I do not recall having seen Colonel Benton there [Benton had placed troops to guard the home on September 10], and we never saw any guards about the place at any time. The troops were orderly and committed no lawlessness that I am aware of. People went about their business, etc., in an ordinary, unmolested manner.
Yvon Pike to Fay Hempstead, 1926

Silas seems to have had a different experience. Silas's son wrote his father's non-endearing Confederate duty was to "confiscate food and feed, if necessary, anywhere it could be found," including others' hogs. Silas went into the war, whole hog, and prided himself the rest of his life as un-reconstructed. His son's apocryphal, unreconstructed version, written 90 years later, conveniently omits cousin Will, and instead features Silas bravely standing up to an arrogant Negro Union officer, and, dubiously, having $10,000 in gold.

I was born there August 3, 1868, three years after the close of the Civil War, the seventh of my father's 12 children, all born in this home ... three brothers older than I, my brothers ranging from 10 to 18 years older. They were old enough to know much about the war ... and Father too told me personally. Before the war Father was known as the leading and largest merchant in Arkansas. They were but few businesses in Little Rock at that time, as the state was young and the town small. When the war was declared, Father joined the Confederate Army, and because of his business qualifications and experience was soon made a captain in the commissary corps, the hardest and most difficult place in the army to feed the army and the horses ... provided at any cost, and in any manner possible. Gold and silver money was scarce, so the Southern army printed and supplied ... with Confederate money. His duty was to confiscate food and feed, if necessary, any place it could be found ... (then) Confederate money became worthless and had no value. This caused my father to become very unpopular among those who have been forced to give up their goods for money that became of no value in the South. General Steele's Army captured Little Rock, causing ... move to Washington, in Hempstead County. The state capital ... too. The war was still on, and the Army had to be fed and .... The Federal Army occupied the ...best houses. This included our old home which our family had evacuated. In time, the Federal Army (moved on) leaving some troops as guards.... Father was glad to leave Hempstead County with his family.... General Steele gave Father permission to occupy one room.... A Negro lieutenant was still in possession. He was very arrogant and insulting, which Father disliked. They got into an

argument and the officer drew his sword and made for
Father. ...picked up a piece of stove wood and hit the Negro
on the head, so again he had to run away ... the government
confiscated his house, for striking an officer. Later he bought
it back ... paying them $10,000 in gold for it. As Captain in
the Commissary Department, Father got all the blame ...
Father brought his army trunk home... A heavy canvas cover
was over it and it bore the imprint Captain Silas Feild—
Commissary Corps—Confederate Army.... It was full of new
Confederate paper money which no one wanted. It had no
value then, now, or ever will—only a sad remembrance. The
Army pistols, rifles, and shotgun ... besides much bitterness
that may never end. Father would not allow me to own a U.S.
flag. He was a good Confederate soldier to the end. Hoping
this information is a value to others I am your loving dad.
William A Feild (1868-1957), 1956.

The Bros and the Silas side of the family at some point parted
ways. No one ever explained why. Perhaps no one remembered.
Perhaps Will was just fine with Yankee dollars and moved past
"much bitterness that may never end."

The Confederates left under a cloud of defeat and civil disorder.
The Yankees, of whom the Bros had heard no good, were not just in
town, but in their home. They were now old enough to form impressions. The 24/7 presence of the enslaved members of the households,
and the care and feeding they provided, were gone. Will, peacefully,
profitably, and immediately began co-existing with Federals. The tight
times of War replaced with plenty, with the reopening of river traffic
and Will's growing inventory. An increase in population was visible
at a time when so much of life was lived in public on the streets.
Ragged, ill-fed, and undisciplined Confederates were replaced by uni-
formed Federals, including African American troops. And then a
return of Southern ragged, ill-fed veterans, around the corner from
811. A sizeable contingent tasked to keep civil order arrived.

"Took up our present quarters in the Capitol building...city very pretty, finely situated, lighted with gas, water pure, and location healthy. Communication with "outside" once opened will be perfect. 23 officers, 350 men Union Provost Guard. The people generally are glad that Rebel rule has ended. The shameless skedaddle of General Price has greatly lessened their confidence in southern chivalry, and they are ready to give up the contest. Their money was already good for nothing—now it's an insult to offer it. Prices have reached unheard of rates: flower $200 per barrel, coffee $12, sugar $1.50 a pound, etc. There are many union men who are overjoyed, I assure you."
Seargent Major Hale, Third Regiment
Weekly Pioneer and Democrat, Oct 16, 1863

Refugee Relief Committee for the State of Arkansas: Being in a shanty at the southwest part of town, not far from Mr. Silas Feild—8 in the family and 6 of them sick, no provisions except a little corn bread....no means of support and no medicine, my impressions the simple truth is that they are starving to death....
(signed) ES Peak, Chaplain U.S. Volunteers
Little Rock Unconditional Union, July 1864

In January 1864, the same year WP and Ernest enrolled at St. John's College, David O'Dodd, age 17 years, two months, a trained telegraph operator, was arrested departing Little Rock carrying details in Morse code of Little Rock troop positions hidden in his shoe. He was armed with a derringer. While awaiting hanging, he was already Boy Martyr of the South. He was captured in civilian clothes, and under military law, that fatal attire made him a spy. Had he, as a student at the College, worn his St. John's cadet uniform, would it have saved his life?

Once again, crowds streamed south past 811. He was hanged as a spy on St. John's grounds. The estimated 6,000 witnesses and then mourners, the majority from outside the town, arrived weeping or surly or both. The events were but tersely noted by a Union soldier. The weather being a bigger factor than his spelling or a hanging.

Clear and Cold, the air keen and Sharp this morning. In the woods chopping firewood today the ice five inches and a half thick here. A rebel spi hung hear today at 3 o'clock by the name of David O. Dodd. It thawed a little today on the South side of the hills, but it is freezing hard to night.
L G Hall Diary, January 8, 1864

The body was taken to a Mr Knighten's front porch on Rock Steet for a viewing by the public.

Albert Pike, Yvon's father, knew Rush through his law practice and as a neighbor "considered him the best-read lawyer he had ever met" reflecting his Virginia law school training. Pike did not occupy the home after the Occupation. His reputation suffered after atrocities by Native American CSA troops under his command at the Battle of Pea Ridge in NW Arkansas...

"8 scalped and others were horribly mutilated."
Report of the Joint Committee on the Conduct of the War:
Bull Run-Ball's Bluff

The Confederate Cavalry Generals' duel had proven folly and death away from battle. The Union leadership contributed to solo folly and death.

"General Steele had given a party ... champagne and other liquids flowed freely ... regardless of the fact that it was the Sabbath ... After dinner, Colonel Manter ordered his horse

and orderly, proposing a ride to the home of a prominent citizen ... prided himself upon being the finest horseman in Steele's army; six feet high in his stockings, with an Apollo figure... the day being beautiful, and the streets crowded, a fine opportunity for display was presented. It so happened that a cow was lying on the street, there being no city ordinance prohibiting either cow or hogs from running at large in that city. In a moment of unaccountable folly, (he) attempted the foolish feat of making his splendid charger jump the cow. Putting his spurs into the horse the animal started to leap at once, but the cow sprang up so suddenly that Colonel Manter was thrown violently ... upon his head, and breaking his neck.... Thus died, from an act of folly, the man whom rumor said, was the controlling spirit of the commanding general, his mouthpiece and most confidential adviser.
The Forty-third Regiment of Indiana Volunteers.
An Historic Sketch of Its Career and Services, 1903

The war would last another 19 months. Arkansas men remained in the field, fighting and still dying, for a Confederacy that had offered in defense of the state and Little Rock only a slow fighting retreat, then a skeedaddle. Bros experienced the occupation at close range, including military pomp and bravado, suffering and death, and soldiers and veterans lacking eyes, arms, or legs. The contrast of simultaneous ruin of war and return of shipping and order was striking.

Sanitary Condition of the City.
We would call the attention of the authorities to the sanitary condition of the city, which is now nothing more nor less than one vast camp. ... streets and allies (sic) are in a very filthy condition, and from the odors which strike our olfactories as we pass certain premises... also in an unwholesome condition. With all the care which can be

taken, disease will prevail here as warm weather advances.
All filth should be removed from the entire city and
disinfecting agents used, if the health of the citizens and
soldiers is regarded.
Little Rock Unconditional Union, May 13, 1864

At the same time, luxury and leisure resumed.

Messrs Eaton & Co., will respectfully inform the public that
they have opened a first class Ice Cream and Refreshment
Saloon on Markham Street, next square east of the Post
Office, where they are prepared to attend to the wants of
both Ladies and Gentlemen, in the best of style. They will
also furnish ice cream to families and parties, on the shortest
notice. Finely furnished rooms for the accommodation of
Ladies open Sundays. Give us a call."
The Unconditional Union, May 1864

Will was now a merchant conveniently alongside the Post
Commissary, U.S. Army, on Markham by the end of 1863.

The town was now flooded with U.S. greenbacks, the Arkansas
River was open all the way to New Orleans and the upper
Mississippi and Ohio Rivers. Goods and greenbacks flowed. The
state would not be readmitted to the Union for another five years.

With living arrangements of enslavement gone, and the influx
of Freedmen and Freedwomen, came a housing crisis. Union forces
established areas, a site Blissville, east of the State Capitol, and a
new area west of Broadway, just south of Mount Holly Cemetery,
on Ninth Street. The Ninth Street community would flourish for
almost 100 years.

As the CSA departed, they left behind 1,400 sick and wounded
in a hospital at St. John's College. The Federals expanded the hospital to 11 ward buildings that would care for a total of over 11,000
patients. Dysentery led the way, hitting armies without choosing

sides, alongside injuries from muskets, bayonets, artillery, and fallen horses. If not immediate, death, demise, or recovery could proceed at a slow pace. Day and night, the Arsenal shared with the town the cries of amputations and probing of wounds for bullets, the screams of shattered bodies being shifted, pleas for loved ones, for help, and the stench of gangrene, dysentery, rows of open privies, animal waste, and pus. Bugles marked the early morning, dusk, and lights out, as well as sounding orders during the day. Heating, cooking, boiling water, all were wood fired and the smoke added to the atmosphere. Across the town, all would have heard Federals and Freedmen, with axes and saws, leveling acres of timber for fortifications, clearing fields of fire to prevent a Confederate counterattack that never came. By late 1864 though, it was clear Little Rock was firmly held and the engineering work stopped, though the local landscape was marked by defensive preparations visible at least until 1908. The Federal presence was everywhere.

The African American population of Little Rock grew rapidly as a life in town, and hoped-for support of the Freedman's Bureau beckoned. In 1860, 23 percent of Little Rock citizens were African American; by 1870, it was 43 percent.

In late 1863, Unionist Clubs arose. By January 1864, Isaac Mills, the former Know Nothing, now a Unionist, traveled to DC as a member of a self-appointed delegation of five and met with President Lincoln, seeking return to the Union. They made their case. After the meeting, the President sent instructions to Steele to establish civil government. Also, a March 28 election would choose a Governor, precluding the appointment of a military governor. On return, they were reviled, especially the delegation in general, and E.W. Gant specifically, a secessionist who became embittered.

We have no fraternity with the likes of him. They might have saved themselves the trouble. There are enough federal soldiers now in the state to make up 1/10 of the

Isaac was rewarded with a Presidential appointment and Senate confirmation as U.S. Marshal for the Eastern District in 1866, and in 1872 he was again appointed a Federal Land Agent, all secure, salaried Federal positions. He openly supported Freedmen and literacy.

We, the undersigned, respectfully recommend taking
favorable consideration of all those to whom these presents
shall come, Mr. Tabs Gross, who proposes to visit the
northern states for the purpose of soliciting aid in behalf of
the Arkansas Freeman, a newspaper established and now
being conducted by Mr. Gross, in the city of Little Rock, and
being devoted especially to the interests of the colored
people of Arkansas.
Powell Clayton, Governor of Arkansas, Robert J.T. White,
Secretary of State, A.K. Hartman, Mayor of the City of
Little Rock, Isaac C. Mills, U.S. Marshal (and four others)
Arkansas Gazette, December 16, 1869

While Mills was working as a Unionist, Will now advertised, the "highest market price cotton." A bale weighed about 500 pounds, and an acre could yield one to one and a half bales. He later reported an income of $429 for 1864. The next year was better. In October 1865, he recorded sales of cotton, taxed at $438.64. For 1865, he also paid Federal taxes for businesses as a retail dealer, real estate agent, and a wholesale dealer, and in 1866, as commercial broker. The groundwork was laid for the Bros' future ventures.

With emancipation, occupation, and the Reconstruction Lincoln intended, town government functioned, taxing and issuing bonds of uncertain value. Will and Sam accepted them at face value and began rebuilding trade.

List of Merchandise Tax under oath for the quarter ending
June 30, 1866, in the city of Little Rock, as shown by the
collectors list published by direction of the city authorities
Feild & Dolley, $8,000,* W H Feild, $741
CITY BONDS will be received by
FEILD AND DOLLEY
For merchandise at cash prices
NO DISCOUNT
WHOLESALE OR RETAIL
Arkansas Gazette, June 1867
[*$8,000 would be worth $150,000 in 2021.]

The town grew and construction boomed.

New Advertisements
Lumber! Lumber!
I have a large amount of lumber on hand and fill orders
without delay at prices to compete with other mills. Messrs
Feild and Dolley, Ditter building will attend promptly to all
orders left with them.
J.H. TRUNDLE
PALAM MILL
Arkansas Gazette, August 1867

Incongruously, in Arkansas where many lived by bare subsistence, Will's store's array of goods exposed the family to the wider world and luxuries. Five years after Occupation and three years after peace, he and Sam Dolley were selling some of everything.

FEILD AND DOLLEY
At their new brick store home, Ditter Block, 194 Markham St,
Little Rock. Arkansas
Are now receiving a large and well selected stock of new
goods fresh from the eastern markets. All the latest styles and
fashions of Ladies' and Gentlemen's plain and fancy dress
goods, staple and fancy dry goods, clothing, hats, caps,
boots and shoes for all, notions in great variety, carpets of all
grades and patterns, and leather goods, spun thread, cotton
cards, willow, wood and hollow ware, hardware., cutlery and
queenware of all kinds, groceries and plantation supplies, all
the substantials and luxuries of the market, with many other
desirable articles they are selling at unusually low prices for
CASH. The ladies and country merchants are especially
invited to call, examine and price, that they may be convinced.
FEILD & DOLLEY
Arkansas Gazette, September 1868

Congress rejected Lincoln's intent and enacted Radical Reconstruction, with martial law, and a requirement for Statehood to include ratification of the 14th Amendment. The State Constitution of 1868 offered progress, mandating public schools for all, segregated. The Fifth Arkansas Constitution of 1874 replaced it, backsliding on that progress, especially for Freedmen. While the U.S. Constitution has existed for 231 years with 27 amendments, Arkansas's 1874 document has been amended 102 times as of 2020, though from 1918 to 1979, three state constitutional conventions submitted replacements. None were adopted.

IX.
Sharp Practice, Handshakes, U.S. Supreme Court

Pappaw used the derisive term "sharp practice" to mean questionable or shady business practices. Certain business practices by Will seem to fit that. What did the Bros learn from this? To allow the reader to look over the shoulders of both parties and the courts, and pass judgment on the legendary handshake and that a man's word is his bond, here are excerpts from the U.S. Circuit and Supreme Court records, including transcribed testimony and letters. Note, Will's lawyer was Augustus Garland, predictor of Arkansas being the "weakest state in the cotton Confederacy."

In October 1865, Will went to Memphis and put his entire annual crop into the hands of Farrington & Howell, an established firm of cotton factors, i.e., brokers. He told them to "sell; cotton bringing not less than 50 cents a pound." The very next day, he telegraphed "do not sell my cotton till I see you. [The] market [is] excited, and higher than at any subsequent time." Will soon returned to Memphis and requested "an advance [on his cotton] of $11,000…very nearly if not quite equal to its value." From there, he took the train east after telling them the lot was "to be sold at their discretion, but he expressed great confidence in higher prices." On his return trip, he stopped in Memphis to see them and "approved of not selling" and said he would appreciate it and remember it in the future. The market was "declining and the firm justified in their action in not selling." In the face of their quite large advance, Farrington stated "that Mr. Feild was always represented to them as entirely solvent and able to pay his debts, and that they wished to follow his own views."

In his testimony, Will stated he gave "express instructions to sell within ten days," and to reimburse themselves for the money advanced. "Cotton had declined one cent on the pound. I remonstrated with them for not having sold. They excused theselves [as] only having been acting for my interest, which excuse I accepted. I, however, renewed my instructions, and the last words I said to Mr. Farrington, on shaking hands with him, were these: 'Whatever you do, do not let the cotton fall one cent lower.'"

But handshake or not, from there it was as muddy as the Mississippi River.

Memphis, November 16th, 1865

Dear Sir [Feild]: We have not sold. [The] market has been dull and on the decline every day since you left. The dispatches from New York yesterday quote middling cotton about 50 cents and very dull. The public dispatches quote 50 at 51 cents, while the private give 49 at 50 cents. Your cotton would not, in the present market, sell here for over 43 or 44 cents. As the money market is very tight, *we will be compelled to sell your cotton unless you make other shipments or remit us as a margin in cash.* We have held on thus far to meet your views, but the declining tendency of the market induces us to write this letter. *Please to let us hear from you on receipt.*

In court, Will acknowledged he received their letter, but decided they were now on the hook for the entire transaction.

"I was surprised to learn that the cotton had not been sold. I thought the plaintiffs had made themselves liable by their neglect to sell. *I was afraid to answer their letter, as I regarded it as a mere endeavor to obtain some admission or concession from me; and I concluded to abandon the matter, leaving them with whatever responsibility they might have incurred. Cotton had fallen in the market,* and I did not feel disposed to make myself a party to their delinquency."

Nine months later in August of 1866, Farrington tried again.

"We are astonished at not hearing from you.... We wrote you ... but have heard nothing.... This was many months ago. *When you left your cotton here, you were not satisfied with the market, although that was about 50c....* On your return, you approved of our efforts and *that the cotton had not been sold.*
"The price has greatly declined, and the expenses have been going on. *Now let us hear your views.* The cotton will not pay your account, as you know, ... and we ask you to remit us for the balance. According to the present market, the cotton would be well sold at 32c (with tax).
We have now *waited to meet your views* until it is necessary for something to be done.... *Write us on receipt of this, for we are anxious.* Very respectfully,
FARRINGTON & HOWELL"

Cotton having gradually declined 30 cents a pound, they wrote again on September 12th, 1866, that they now "despaired hearing of Mr. Feild, who appeared to us to have abandoned it and had no intention of assuming the control of it, or of paying us the amount he owed us.... I had but one wish to act in a manner for Feild."

Will was advised "the sale was at the highest [market]," and the "firm would send account sales and account as soon as the cotton was delivered." Again he did not respond.

In September 1866, the cotton was finally sold, and Will was billed for the balance of $6,695. "Feild took no notice ... refused payment."

In December of 1869, the Supreme Court passed no judgment on sharp practices, but did fault the trial judge's instructions to the jury. Justice William Strong wrote the opinion: "Reversed, and a new trial ordered. Feild v Farrington."

Seven years after the original transaction...

"US District Court
Farrington & Howell v WH Feild. Settled by agreement and dismissed at defendant's cost."
Arkansas Gazette, April 1872

No handshake recorded.

It is not a world record, but having a case in both U.S. and Arkansas Supreme Courts at the same time bears mention.

That same month, Will borrowed money from a Mr. Shall to pay taxes on land he owned at a usurious two percent per month on April 1, 1872. (An April Fool joke?)

"If obligation is given for money, advanced to pay my taxes for the year 1871. The tax lien given by law on my property, for which this money was advanced to pay taxes, I hear by recognize, witnessed my hand and seal, WH Fld."

In the interim, Shall died, and a Mr. Peay became executor. Will filed for bankruptcy, and Shall had no lien on Feild's property. If a joke, Shall's heirs were the punchline.

X.

Brothers and Town
Begin to Come of Age

Brooks it is said provided himself a copy of this (Court's)
judgement.... went to the executive office and ejected Gov.
Baxter by force. Gov. Baxter immediately telegraphed the
situation to the President ... and has issued his proclamation
declaring martial law in the county of Pulaski.
Arkansas Gazette, April 1874

The Boys ... one of the prominent dancing clubs ... crowded
... dancing to the beautiful music of the Italian Band ...
accompanied by Gov daughter on piano.
Arkansas Gazette, December 1877

On schedule, in 1869, the U.S. transcontinental railroad was complete. The Little Rock-to-Memphis line opened in 1872. A reporter made the trip from Memphis to Little Rock.

"Before you start, get a bottle of medicine for sea sickness. It
is certainly the most remarkable railroad in the United States,
and worth seeing by anyone whose nerves are so steady,

and courage is tolerably good. Running straight through the Lost Swamp, the railroad is sometimes entirely overflowed by a rise in the river, other times sinks into the oozy mud and disappears altogether."

"At sunset, we reached Little Rock, thankful that we had done as well as to accomplish 138 miles since light in the morning, and were not sticking in the swamp overnight, the fate of many less fortunate travelers."
New York Tribune, August 15, 1872

His train derailed three times en route.

The Little Rock School District organized the same year and a first newspaper reference to the Fighting Alley appeared, a square block, wide open, on the riverfront, with saloons, prostitutes, and crime, including murders.

Samuel Dolley never married, but was a part of an extended family from Yell County, as well as the Little Rock family and friends. He watched the Bros grow and mature. His 1871 death at home at 227 Main dissolved the Feild and Dolley partnership, and Silas served as administrator of his estate, but business continued under the same name until the Panic of 1873, which lasted through 1879. Federal paper greenbacks, without gold backing from the Civil War, plus more railroad bonds, the bubbles all burst. Economists and the press labeled the Panic as the The Depression; however in 1929, that title went to the 1929 Crash, and 1874 was demoted to the Long Depression. Credit from wholesalers and to customers dried up. Bankruptcy. The store went to Mr. N. Marshall, whose earlier arrival as a salesman at the store had been widely advertised as a coup. The transaction was friendly, and a young WP was soon working there as a clerk.

The 1872 Governor's contest was contentious, amidst myriad balloting irregularities. The ultimate victor, if not numerical winner, was Republican scalawag Elisha Baxter from Batesville who had served in the Union Army and was elected by the Legislature to the U.S. Senate the same time as Grandpa Hunter. He defeated Carpetbagger Joseph Brooks, an Ohioan, who came to Arkansas as a Federal Chaplain. One month before the election, Grandpa Hunter's name, maybe by his own encouragement or not, was briefly in the race as a Liberal Republican, with supporters expecting him to displace Brooks. The leading men of the state, and young men, risked their fortunes on Mr. Hunter's success.

Grandpa Hunter quickly withdrew his name on the grounds he had never been formally consulted nor had he consented. Ultimately his reputation remained intact.

No one can question Mr. Hunter's integrity for his short lived candidacy, or for declining it.
Arkansas Gazette, October 1872

Two years after the election, Brooks found a friendly judge who declared him the rightful victor in the election. On April 15, 1874, Baxter was with his 10-year-old son who was spending time with him in the office. Brooks and others entered the capitol and physically ejected Baxter from his physical office, and according to them, from his illegally elected office.

One governor settled in to the state house, the other governor, hot-footed it, son in tow, the 10 blocks, past 811, to the St. John's College, snugly and smugly adjacent to the U.S. Arsenal. The St. John's Cadets formed an initial bodyguard. When the Brooks forces directed two cannons squarely at the Baxter forces at Anthony House hotel, Markham and Scott streets, two companies of occupying U.S. Army troops interposed between the two sides. In a three-way standoff among Union troops, Brooks' 1,000 armed men, and Baxter's perhaps 2,000, it is easy to imagine the clatter of arms, and marching men, and the anguished locals cry of "AGAIN?"

Surely Will told the Bros, "Stay out of it." President Grant ultimately settled the matter on May 15, and Baxter retained his office. Brooks was made Postmaster, and perhaps was placated by a plush Federal job. And Federal salary. By the time it was all over, as many as 500 people had been killed. No doubt the affair provided cover for the bloody settling of old and current scores. If Grandpa Hunter had stayed in the race, the electoral outcome likely would have been different, and it is doubtful that a Hunter-Baxter War would have occurred.

The restoration to the Union in 1868 required Negro suffrage and disenfranchised former Confederates. In the aftermath of the Brooks-Baxter crisis and the 1876 Presidential Election, Federal authority began to withdraw while the 1874 Constitution enfranchised the former Confederates.

By 1860, Little Rock Gas Company had built a modern gasworks that operated by heating coal in an enclosed vessel, producing a gas that could be piped and used for streetlamps.

By the terms of their agreement the Meesrs S(laughter) are
to have their gasworks ready to light up the city on the
first of August.
Arkansas Gazette, April 1860

The lights in fact did go out in town. The works shut down for the start of the War and did not function again, with service extended to homes and businesses for lighting, until around 1870. Natural gas was found in Western Arkansas and piped into parts of Little Rock in 1911.

The right to the ballot was guaranteed to all males. The Little Rock 1870 Census was 12,780, with 43 percent African American (as compared to 23 percent in 1860). Only 22 percent of residents or their families had been in town prior to 1860.

When WP and Ernest, along with cousin Ormand, appeared on Arsenal grounds, they were in uniform, but not in Union or Confederate outfits. Ages 14 and 11, they were among approximately 100 enrolled at St. John's as Cadets in "blue uniforms with light blue stripes," "Cadet" and "SJC" school initials emblazoned on brass buttons. Their curriculum was rigorous and their grading and discipline were reported to the public. The July 1868 *Gazette* reported for WP a solid Second-Class Distinction for University Arithmetic and Dictionary-English Language, and a First in Penmanship, and Ernest with Primary Second Distinction for Primary Geography, Grammar, and Mental Arithmetic. "The tuition of paying students will remain, as heretofore, at $50 for the session of 10 months, for all of the collegiate departments, payable quarterly in advance."

Spelling, Reading, Declamation, and Penmanship. One poor fellow's achievement was heralded, "He would have scored a Third had he not been expelled before the close of the session."

The Ladies Seminary three blocks north, offering English, French, piano, guitar, organ, singing, and embroidery/ornamental work, did not specify attire. Women were mostly invisible in news reports until the Ladies' social organizations began to appear— Young Ladies Charity Club in 1879, the following year, Young Ladies Social Club ("music excellent," "the girls pretty, the boys as gallant as ever"), Ladies Sociable Club 1886, and in 1893, the Ladies Columbian Club.

From the front porch of 811, you could throw an ecumenical rock in any direction and hit a religious structure. Congregants would pass to and fro on Friday night, Sunday morning, Wednesday evening. Jewish, Methodist, Presbyterian, Baptist, Episcopalian, Lutheran, and Catholic were all in a four-block radius.

By 1870 on Sundays, 14 churches and the synagogue were gathering somewhere, and English, Latin, Hebrew, and German liturgy and voices could be heard. The synagogue, which did not have services, did conduct a business meeting on Sunday mornings. Start times varied from 10 AM, 10:30 AM, 2 PM, 7:30 PM, to 8 PM. By the end of the day, according to the newspapers, a total of 29 opportunities to fill pews were available. The Jewish community was part of the community at large. In 1871, Temple B'nai Israel was built at Center and Third street. The *Gazette* published notices for services for Jewish New Year, Yom Kippur, and Hanukkah, and announced a joint Thanksgiving Day service with the Christian churches.

The secular circus came to town, though no performances were scheduled on Sundays. For two days, Dan Rice's 1873 Paris Pavilion Circus performed directly behind 811, on Cumberland. Rice introduced the phrase "on the bandwagon" by inviting Zachary Taylor to parade from there and advertised "Sensation of the Century." Dan Rice advertised that old maids could visit his show at half price, but he never had a female call for a half-price ticket. With the circus, the Bros were old enough to note ladies in titillating acrobatic costume, rehearsing, and young enough to revel in the backstage of the circus literally in their backyard. Oddly the advertisement has the large drawing of Mr Rice and only hints at the attributes of the acrobats.

Howe's Great London Circus 1875 tour made a stop. Forspaugh's Show attempted to negotiate a decrease in the City license of $100. The City countered with a request for 50-cent admissions instead of 75 cents. The Board voted No, and the show moved outside the City limits.

Bill Lake's "Hippo-Olympiad and Mammoth Circus" played Little Rock and smaller venues from DeValls Bluff to Rockport in Hot Spring County, to Princeton in Dallas County with the 1869 "King Bee Show." Additional shows included Cooper's and Barnum's Circuses in 1872, Welsh and Sands' "Monarch Marvel of All Time" in 1880. As with baseball, the Circus had no show on Sunday, a day of rest.

XI.
FREED MEN AND WOMEN

That on the first day of January, in the year of our Lord, one thousand eight hundred and sixty-three, all persons held as slaves within any State, ... shall be, thenceforward, and forever free; and ... the United States ... will recognize and maintain the freedom of such persons, and will do no act or acts to repress such persons, or any of them, in any efforts they may make for their actual freedom.
Emancipation Proclamation, January 1, 1863

neither slavery nor involuntary servitude ... shall exist within the United States
13th Amendment, 1865

All persons born or naturalized in the United States ... are citizens of the United States and of the State wherein they reside. No State shall make or enforce any law which shall abridge the privileges or immunities of citizens of the United States; nor ... deprive any person of life, liberty, or property, without due process of law; nor deny ... equal protection of the law.
14th Amendment, 1868

The right of citizens of the United States to vote shall not be denied ... on account of race, color, or previous condition of servitude.
15th Amendment, 1870

I give and bequeath to Lucinda Howell, a woman of color and formerly a slave belonging to me,... to have and to hold the said real estate, and personal property, from my death absolutely, together with all the improvements, mills, gin, machinery, and houses.
Last Will and Testament
John Bright Howell, April 28, 1880

I further will that all my negroes (Nancy Excepted) together with all my other personal estate in the County of Chatham aforesaid with my outstanding debts after paying my just debts out of the same be equally divided between my said sisters, their heirs .. as they may agree amongst themselves.
Will of James Anderson, 1793, probated 1795
N.C. State Archives

Nancy was excepted. Possibly, she was Rush's enslaved aunt or first cousin. What were their feelings about slavery? As Edward McGee relates below, Will actively attempted to arrange an armed, escorted trip to Texas to prevent McGee's emancipation. The young single lawyer Rush arrived in Tennessee with, as recorded by the 1820 Census, one "male," "slave," "less than 14 years old." African Americans were legally denied U.S. citizenship, and Arkansas had outlawed just living in the state as a free African American. Once Emancipation was declared, the existing evil was or should have been apparent.

Slave Narratives: A Folk History of Slavery from the WPA Writers Project collected 1936–38 are oft-cited records of the era. There were 696 Arkansas interviewees, but 600 had moved to the state after emancipation. And the WPA interviews were conducted 71 years after the end of the war. The Southern Claims Commission records (1871–1874), contain handwritten verbatim transcripts. These provide first-person accounts from claimants and their supporting witnesses, sworn, but not immediate contemporary accounts.

They give a first-hand account of the city, family, war, occupation, lives enslaved, and the early days of emancipation. The Freedman's Bank (1865–1874) recorded information on customers, family, and daily life.

The Commission consisted of a three-member Board supported by local Special Commissioners who reviewed small claims in local areas and Special Agents who traveled from state to state gathering evidence. The Commission received 22,298 claims for damages totaling $60,258,150.44. It only approved 7,902 claims totaling $4,636,920.69. Its work was declared ended in 1880. Of 55 claims in Pulaski County, 32 received some compensation. The claimants and their witnesses included Freedmen and the white community. Edward McGee, approximately 18 years old at secession, was living—without a last name, and in the Census Slave Schedule not even a first name acknowledged—enslaved and residing in "slave quarters" at the rear of 811. His description of working on his own, and keeping payment for himself, was unusual, though more common in urban areas, and was reported by others in Little Rock.

> In April 1861 I resided in Little Rock. I was a slave and belonged to William H Feild. I lived in Little Rock with the Fields (sic) from that time until just before the Federals came to this place in September. I didn't know what the war was commenced about. After come out (sic) and was going on a long time I knew all about it. A man told me what it was about. Mr. Thomas Johnson told me it was to set the colored people free. I believed him and feel if it was so it made me feel pretty proud. I wanted the federal soldiers to come in. It was the second year of the war

before I knew anything about what the war was for. From that time, I wanted the Union cause to succeed. Yes sir.
Edward McGee
Southern Claims Commission, Record 4294, 1872

In an arrangement that existed in some more urban areas in the South, by 1863 …

I made a power of it [money]. I paid him my master $100 a month. A man could make $400 a month. That here was plenty of it…. I was draying and made a good deal of Confederate money and got silver with it paying $5 dollars (Confederate) for $1 (U.S.). I thought Confederate money would die out. I thought so because the Federals might come this way.

And he was right, the Confederate money was soon worthless, again echoing 1861, Stillwell and Garland, "without hope of ever being stronger."

Tens of thousands, maybe a hundred thousand, of enslaved people were taken to Texas after Emancipation was made public.

Not all arrived.

I was starting to Texas with other slaves…. A white man named James Jim Meadow had charge of the gang of us. He never got any there for we went to the Federals and brought them to him. They took him to Danville and took his stock (six mules) And that bottle him up from going anywhere…. Seven of us ran away in Yell County, Arkansas, to the Federals … went with them to Danville, Yell County, Arkansas, and then came to Little Rock and the Federal Army was here thick. I then remained in Little Rock until the close of the War until the present time was draying for myself until my horses were taken, and then I drayed for another man.

Later, a man named James Meadows while hunting in White County "accidentally shot himself, in the left arm, amputated above the elbow." (*Arkansas Gazette*, January 1870)

If it was the same fellow, McGee could be forgiven for wishing for a mortal wound, or at least his right arm.

Slaves were moved against their will, but slaveholders also moved, though of their own volition, leaving the enslaved behind, but still not free. Daniel Cooke, another witness:

> "I lived with a brother of claimant's master (Silas, Ninth and Cumberland SW corner) a few months before the Federals came because my master run."

Edward McGee returned to town a Freedman, with a last name of his choice, free to marry, and no threat of separation from loved ones by sale. He had the means to support a family, working his team of mules and wagon. He married, his wife, named Mattie, had a household of eight, including his brother, sister-in-law, and nieces. In 1865, Edward McGee's two horses were taken by the Union wagon master Buck Stanton, a civilian. He signed his Claim with his mark, "X." The 1870 census recorded he could read, but not write.

> In the case of Edward McGee ...
> claimant expects to prove that the witness was present with the claimant when the two horses were taken from the stable in use by claimant and that the horses were taken by Buck Stanton in the employ of some quartermaster either as Quartermaster Sergeant or Wagon Master. The witness knows Stanton well and is confident that it was him that took the horses. He heard Stanton tell the claimant something about his getting good pay for his horses when General Steele came back. He told claimant that he had an order to take all the horses he could find as the Army needed to them.

A witness for McGee, Charles James:

McGee did not own those horses before the Federals came. He bought them directly after they got in, I think he used to haul wood.... I was not present when they were taken. A good many colored man in Little Rock owning (sic) horses and mules and it was a time of distress among us and I meet up with claimant in the street.

IN THE MATTER OF THE CLAIM OF EDWARD MCGEE (COLORED)
... property in question, was taken from or furnished by Edward ...for use of a portion of the Army of the United States known as (blank) and commanded by Major General Fred Steele and that the person who took or received the property or who authorized it or directed it to be taken or furnished were the following. Buck Stanton quartermaster department or wagon master is in the employ of the quarter master that the property was removed to quartermaster stables in Little Rock and used for or by the quartermaster and handling of general work. On or about the 20th day of April in the year 1864 it appears by the petition presented to the Commissioners.

Freedman Beaver Washington also met Buck Stanton. He was also a claimant, for a mule and dray harness. He also was denied. Not every claim nor every Freedman was denied, nor did they all blame Buck. Freedman Tarlton Hardin had a bay horse taken by soldiers. His claim for $150 was allowed but paid at $60. Luke Tucker with Beaver Washington had his claim allowed for $200. One (white) witness supported his claim, but ... McGee submitted a claim for $150 for the two horses, taken by the Union, but it was denied. The war brought an end to his enslavement, but at a cost of more than his horses.

"My brothers—Thomas and Robert and Christopher—were in the Federal army. 11th U.S. Colored Infantry. Thomas and Robert are living now, one in Memphis and one of them upriver about 2 miles. Christopher died in the service."

In all, there were 5,562 colored troops from Arkansas. McGee, Beaver Washington, James Jackson, Jackson Brown, Solomon Winfrey, et al were hurt by seizure of working stock used to support families, accumulate capital, and to establish themselves as citizens.

Solomon Winfrey (1829–1902) was helpful to many fellow Freedmen, and his name appears in the records of several claims. He did hauling through the occupation, moved on to brick masonry and plastering, and became successful as a contractor, with four houses and other property. In 1879, his daughter Cora married J. E. Bush, co-founder of the National Order of the Mosaic Templars. Bush was a school master and in 1898 appointed by President McKinley as by Receiver of United States Lands Office, Little Rock. In 1911, he was worth an estimated $100,000 ($3 million in 2021). By 1942, his family home, 1500 Chester, was the 20-bed Lena Jordan Hospital.

McGee must have been very good with horses: 1899 "Lbr Arkansas Stables, living Broadway." In 1912, McGee was still in transportation, "(c) Tmstr" (colored teamster), 1915 as a "(c) lab" (colored laborer) with Merchants Transfer Co, living at 600½ W. Markham. The Federals had brought emancipation, the War had cost him a brother, and Buck Stanton had taken his team and wagon. He had lived on the grounds of 811 as the Bros grew up. Later, as they all moved about town, did they greet one another? And if so, how?

In 1865, Congress chartered the Freedman's Bank and Trust to serve the emancipated. Little Rock had a branch. Accounts were available for Freedmen, but also for white depositors as well. The records of accounts opened, like those of the Southern Claims Commission, demonstrate the Lost Cause falsehoods of the helpless in need of the kindly supervision of benevolent masters. Depositors were identified by name and *reductio ad absurdum* efforts to describe customers by "complexion": "nearly white," "brown-light," "medium," "very light," "yellow," "mulatto.'"And simply "white." But they also recorded employment, employer, if any, date and place of birth and raising, residence, age, occupation, spouse, children, father, mother, and siblings. Individuals of all ages, including young children, had accounts. Occupations of African Americans were listed such as seamstress, porter, gardener, washerwoman, pastor, blacksmith, well digger, apprentice, barkeeper, hotel steward, grocer, school teacher, servant, night watchmen, penitentiary guard, waiter, saddler, painter, printer, deputy City Marshal, cordwood cutter, brick mason, nurse, boot black, news carrier, policeman, legislator, man of all work, machinist, gas fitter, skiff boatman, barber, drayman, and seamstress. Under remarks, listed some poignant agency such as "works for himself," "work for no one," "will work for anybody," and the proud "nobody."

Freedman church congregations and benevolent organizations opened accounts for saving and for accountability. Bethel AME Church had several—Wilberforce University, Widows & Orphans Fund, Children's Fund, and their Ladies Church Aid Society. There were also the Preachers Fund, Arkansas Conference AME, and a fund for the men's benevolent society, the Sons of Honor. The effects of the Long Depression were reaching Arkansas. The 1874 assets of the Little Rock Bank were estimated at $200,000, which in 2023 is equivalent to $5 million. The Freedman's Bank continued promises. Poor management and sporadic oversight by Congress, along with the Depression of 1873 that took down Feild and Dolley, led to failure of the bank. The rewards of hard work and saving, along with the promse of some security, capital, and a better future, disappeared. Whites and Freedmen both were hit beyond a bank account.

Will's in laws had settled in Yell County, the Jamesons in 1836, and Howells 1820. Mary Rebecca's Howells side of the family were from North Carolina. Her grandfather, Stephen Howell, had two sons, her father James and his brother John. He likely fathered a half sister, the mother an enslaved woman. His will directed that all the enslaved persons in his estate be sold, except for Harriet. All the local Howells held enslaved people, a total of 39 including 24 children under age 18. Her uncle John Howell (1814–1893) owned 3,000 acres in west Arkansas. His wife Eliza Heard (1824–1842) and family had arrived in western Arkansas in the 1820s. Eliza died, probably related to childbirth, at age 18. Their only son (1842–44) died two years later. John subsequently entered into a relationship with Lucinda, an enslaved women. Since she was enslaved, she had no legal ability to consent. Perhaps Lucinda had nursed the son after Eliza's death. The relationship between John and Lucida endured decades past Emancipation. She lived as Lucinda Howell; all their children had the surname Howell.

In his 1880 will, John left the bulk of the estate in Yell County properties and "all moneys … horses, mules, cattle, wagons, harness, farming and cooking utensils, mills, gin, machinery, and houses" to Lucinda Howell (1825–1895) and 13 others, all with the Howell surname. He identified each as "a person of color and my former slave." He also left 80 acres to his half-sister, "Harriet Jackson a former slave belonging to my mother and who nursed her in old age."

The 1870 Census shows her as head of her own household, with the occupation of a house servant, and unable to read or write. At the next Census, she was still the head of household. Neither she nor her three grandsons attended school. By 1880, all could read and write. She died in 1895 and was buried in the Howell Cemetery in Danville. The same year he wrote the will, Howell referred to himself as a widower. Their children were their flesh and blood, their only heirs, shared his name—family, but not acknowledged.

An extensive biography of John did not mention Lucinda, Harriet Jackson, or the many other Howells beyond Eliza and child. The following may be a sideways judgment of the unspoken.

"He was not connected with any church."
1891 Biographical and Historical Memoirs of Yell County

Howell wrote,

"a slave belonging to me ... to have and to hold the said real estate, and personal property, from my death Absolutely"

"To have and to hold...real estate," "from my death absolutely" but not till death us do part.

Her Will divided personal items, and furniture. A cryptic bequest was to her grandson:

"I give and bequeath to Leslie Howell, son of Hampton Howell, the bed, bedstead, and all the clothing thereto belonging, which was once occupied and used by Capt JB Howell Sr in his lifetime."

WP left personal records of his dealings with the son of a Freedman. Was he his barber?

"Louis McCain (col) barber." The connection that led to the personal financial assistance is unknown. McCain had made the news, both as a member of the Colored Barbers Association, but also shooting at (and missing) a streetcar conductor. He was subsequently pardoned by the Governor, but was then arrested in a raid while shooting craps and paid a $10 fine. In the process of buying and selling barbering equipment, WP made several personal loans to McCain for amounts of $3 and $20 ...

"at a rate of 10 percent per annum until paid ... a lien upon the furniture and fixtures of a barber shop owned by us at 511½ Main" cosigned by McCain and his barber employer.

McCain was also a trial witness in a Jim Crow-style Main Street, broad daylight murder in response to a "loud tone" and "crowding" the sidewalk.

> Reedy Vance killed the Negro soldier John H Jones on Main Street at the corner of Main and Second.... Hobbs, Constable, detailed ... how Vance happened to accompany him in the quest for a negro ... wanted for a felony ... a negro across the street hailed them in a loud tone.... Hobbs remarked the negro ought to be taken in as he seemed to be looking for trouble. .... the Negro crowded two ladies to the edge of the sidewalk and walked to south on Main a short distance and stopped. Addressed to them in an insulting way and called them a vile name. Just then Vance said something and the Negro replied to some effect directing his attention, "You had better go on, nobody is bothering you." The Negro seem to be reaching for his gun and Vance fired. Louis McCain, colored, was in front of Sol Johl's saloon.... he heard no words. Vance gave bond and was released. Jones enlisted ... a few weeks ago at Fort Roots ... was to have been assigned to one of the regular negro regiments.
> *Arkansas Gazette*, December 1898

Vance was acquitted and went on to kill four more men, and shoot one other in a saloon he owned. That victim did not pay for a bowl of soup. Vance served prison time for his last shooting of a "chinaman" trying to collect four cents. He opened a store across the road from Cummins Prison upon release and was killed by a shotgun during a robbery.

A Family Album

Rev. Andrew "Gpa Hunter" Hunter, born in 1813 in Ballymoney, County Antrim, Northern Ireland, died in 1901 in Little Rock, Arkansas

Baby basket made by resident of Feild Brothers Farm, circa 1921 (now at the Historic Arkansas Museum). This is the woven basket that started me on this book project.

Silas Feild home. Entire block of Cumberland from 9th to 10th Street, facing east. (Courtesy of Roberts Library)

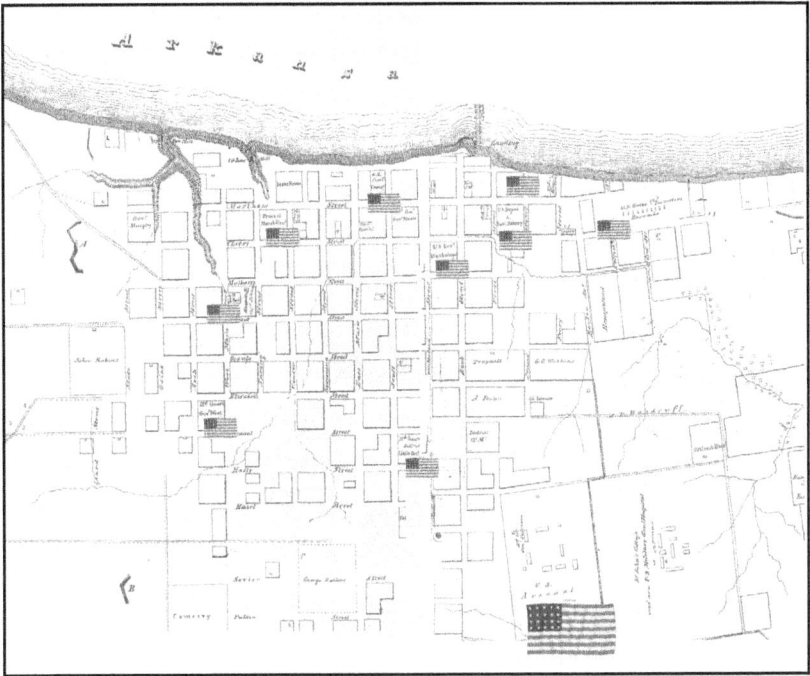

Federal offices and facilities in Little Rock, 1864 (Library of Congress)

WH Feild and Co, handily located next to the Army Commissary, 1863 (Arkansas Heritage Commission)

(Above) U.S.
Arsenal, Army
Band concert,
circa 1865

(Right) Out the
back door of 811—
CIRCUS! 1874

PARIS PAVILION

CIRCUS!

The most stupendous arenic organization
of modern times! The triumph of the season!
The sensation of the century! The nation's
Stars! In one grand combination under the
largest Circus tent in America.

DAN RICE,

Who has spent thirty-six years in securing the leading ACRO-
BATS, GYMNASTS, EQUESTRIANS and TRAPEZE PER-
FORMERS—Male and Female—is now on his grand Western
and Northern tour with a Company

Organized to Conquer!

In the language of the New
Orleans Press, it is the

MODEL CIRCUS

OF AMERICA,

Whether viewed for its gran-
deur, the magnitude and merit
of its performance, the beauty and brilliancy of its vast amphi-
theatre, or the comfort of its patrons.

FIFTY ARTISTS in one Company, with twenty-two of the
most beautiful ring horses on either continent.

Dan Rice's Celebrated Stud of Performing Horses,

Including the world-renowned BLIND EXCELSIOR Jr., Stephen
A. Douglas, Julia, Rebecca and Attakapas.

For the list of artists, some FIFTY IN NUMBER, see pro-
grammes and small bills.

CORNER CUMBERLAND AND EIGHTH STREETS.

106

(Above) Arkansas
Accidental Base
Ball Club. Foul
Flag Association
Champions in
1875. WP is seated
far right.

(Left) Harrington
"Little Harry" Feild,
1881–1883

Concordia Club, built 1903, 801 Scott Street

The 1905 Little Rock High School football team. Pappaw is second from the left in the back row.

Mills family on Hot Springs outing. Mater is second from right. The only smile is on the third donkey from the left. Apparently, Queen Victoria (far left) on a previously unrecorded trip to Hot Springs came along for the ride, circa 1900.

Front yard of 811. The group is facing east with Scott Street behind them, circa 1910. Mater, second from left. Ernest's daughter-in-law Ruth, second from right. Jones Cottage across the street, now moved to Broadway Street.

Neenie and Granddaddy courting. There is some doubt as to whether there was a horse involved in this photo, as only the buggy is visible.

Neenie and Granddaddy. Mama on her lap, sister Vernal on the right

(Above) Pages from the Farm's
commissary ledger, 1921

(Left) A sales slip from the
commissary, 1923

(Right) 1919 technology.

(Below) Almost everyone was within three blocks of a streetcar stop, with junctions for easy transfer to their destination. No parking problems!

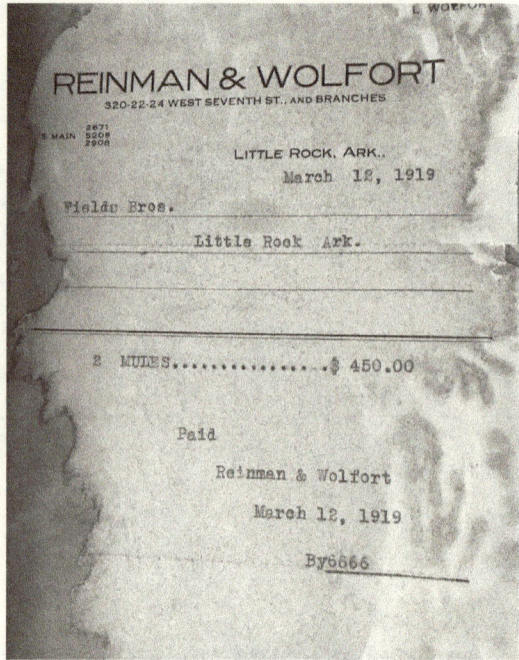

REINMAN & WOLFORT
320-22-24 WEST SEVENTH ST., AND BRANCHES

LITTLE ROCK, ARK.,
March 12, 1919

Fields Bros.

Little Rock Ark.

2 MULES..............$ 450.00

Paid

Reinman & Wolfort

March 12, 1919

By6666

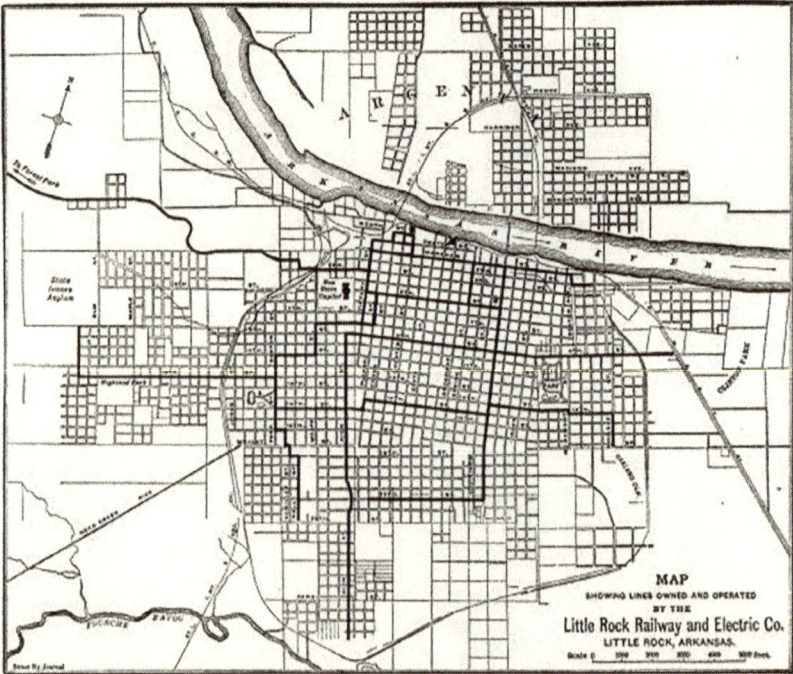

MAP
SHOWING LINES OWNED AND OPERATED
BY THE
Little Rock Railway and Electric Co.
LITTLE ROCK, ARKANSAS.

Cotton Prices: 1914–1944

COTTON PRICE RECEIVED BY FARMERS

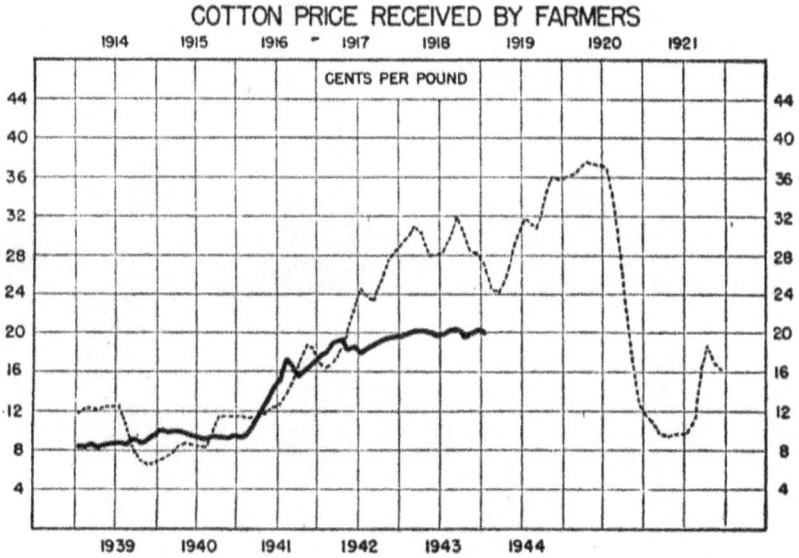

A topsy-turvy world. (Above) Cotton prices during the World Wars (Courtesy of the U.S. Department of Agriculture)

AUTO TURNS TURTLE; FIVE NARROWLY ESCAPE

Presley Feild and Party Receive Only Slight Injuries in Accident Near Sweet Home.

Five persons had a narrow escape from death when a large touring car driven by Presley Feild, 1423 Welch street, skidded into a ditch and turned completely over in a ditch beside the Sweet Home pike, five miles from Little Rock, about 2:30 yesterday afternoon. The members of the party escaped without serious injury.

(Left) Presley and friends survive a different kind of upset.

Daddy with Hezekia "High" Jermany, snow day, circa 1924

Daddy in Paris at the Trocadero, June 1945

Eula Mae holding my sister, with two neighbors, spring 1958

Johnny, Eula Mae's husband, with me on the left. He looks ready to finish his day. Circa 1958

Mater and Pappaw with shoeless neighbors, circa 1965

Feild Bros' final tax bill on the Farm, 1968

XII.

BASEBALL

"The Base Ball Club will meet at St. John's College grounds
on Saturday evening."
Arkansas Gazette, March 1867

Various forms of amusement are here resorted to, for relief
from care and nerve mounting exercise. In front of the stately
Sumter House each evening, when the sun has hid his face
beyond the dark heavy foliage that adorns the picturesque
mountain, there collects a group of athletes and run the rare
sport of baseball; and it would like you to see the invalid
springing nimbly in this athletic diversion and walking
proudly over the lovely front, as though the pallor of disease
had never consumed the flush on his manly cheek.
Hot Springs News, 1867

The Little Rock Ball Club had fielded a team as early as 1857,
but the game was wickets, a form of cricket, rather than what
would later evolve into the modern American game. At a meeting
of the members of the Little Rock Ball Club, on Saturday, the 25th
of April, the following resolution was adopted:

Resolved: A general invitation is hereby extended to the citizens of Little Rock, and the ladies in particular, to attend and see the games of the Club, on Saturday evening next, the second of May, at 3 o'clock....
Arkansas State Gazette and Democrat, May 1857

The first recorded baseball, or base ball, in town was played at the Arsenal. Sam Dolley was Secretary of the Zephyr baseball club. In 1868, as WH Feild and Co Store advertised "Women coarse and medium quality shoes," "Horseshoes and horseshoe nails," "Ladies Cloaks," and "Twenty Barrels Irish Potatoes," an ad that followed

Reardon's Book Store
Chadwick's Game of American Baseball: How to Learn It, How to Play It, How to Teach It
Sponge and Rubber Balls
Arkansas Gazette, December 1868

Chadwick was an Englishman who morphed from cricket reporter to codifying early baseball. Before the telephone, the local press acted as a notice board for the community activities (almost exclusively white and male) and could now include a sport beyond brutal, sometimes fatal boxing, and horse racing centered, around gambling. Local baseball was loosely organized, but the newspaper covered it all. The cheers and jeers and the crack of the bat would, at times, be within earshot of 811.

Today, baseball playing for the fall season will be inaugurated by a match game between the first nine of the Guidon and Galaxy Base Ball Clubs. Let all lovers of this national game be on hand. The players will meet at the Arsenal ground at 2 ½ o'clock p.m. play to be called at three.

BASE BALL—attention Galaxy—there will be a match game of
baseball at the Arsenal grounds this evening between the
Galaxy and Guidon clubs. The following members of the
Galaxy baseball club being chosen by the Board of Directors
to play the match, will please be on the ground at 2 ½ o'clock
to wit: Watkins, English, Pike, Ringo, McHenry, Scott, Weaver,
Hall, and Brody. Play will be called at 3 o'clock precisely
P. D. ENGLISH

Played around the corner from 811, the contest resulted in the
Guidon's win, 64 runs to the Galaxy's 15. The teams were indeed
Clubs, with officers, boards, and business meetings. But first and
foremost, they were also ball teams. That season, the Galaxy Base
Ball Club "Secy and Capt., 1st 9 GBBC," announced a game and
listed his starters by name, instructing, "The following players being
chosen by the board of directors please be on the ground at 2 1/2p."

Four years later, "The game of baseball between the City of
Roses and Actives, both clubs of this city, was not as good as many
expected, the play being unusually loose on both sides." The
Actives fielded WP, Ernest, and Feild cousins Tolly and Arthur,
and won the game by the following scores, Roses–30 runs, 27 outs,
Actives–37 runs and 27 outs.

The Mutuals of Memphis were expected over last night but a
telegram was received late last evening that they could not
come. This will spoil the fun of a good many of our
baseballists who expected a big time today.

Loosely played or not, WP, at short stop, scored two runs and
three outs. Prodigies, WP, at age 15, made the news as a baseball
player, Ernest at age 13. Later, members of the Masonic Fraternity
at St. John's organized the Arkansas Accidentals "Axes" baseball
team. The two older brothers, WP and Ernest, and Silas's boys,

Ormand, Arthur, and Talbot "Tolly" Feild, all played. Silas's son, William A. age five, was Team Mascot. Between 1870 to 1880 at least one Feild played in most local games.

The "Axes" won the Foul Flag League (foul flags preceded a painted foul line) in a 16-game season in 1875. WP, 21 years old, was both player and member of the Axes Board of Directors. An illness later that year, afflicting WP and two Teammates and leading to a canceled game, was reported in the news.

The Axes played the Hot Waters, of Hot Springs; La Roque Base Ball Club, eponymous with their Captain, C.A. LaRoque; the Arsenals; Phenix (sic); and Independents, all of Little Rock. Sports writers were tough on teams, including the Axes. Just before July 4, 1876, the U.S. Centennial, Accidentals lost to Capital City, 25–9.

"Game altogether was a very poor one" ... "Axes were very weak" at bat—the redundant very noted. The hope for the 4th was "a much better and closer game." On a Sunday of Independence Day weekend, Freedmen members of two organized clubs met. "A base-ball match took place yesterday afternoon near Hangerville between clubs composed of colored men. The game was won by the Chain Lightning nine. Going to the ground, the clubs marched in regular order keeping time to the music of a base and snare drum."
Daily Ark Gazette, 5 July 1874

There will be a match game of baseball between the Arlington (Now champions of the state) and Loan Star clubs, 15th and Commerce Street Saturday evening. This being a game for the state championship there is no doubt but that it will be a good match. Both clubs are comprised of colored boys of the city and play well.
Arkansas Gazette, June 1880

And with St. John's, 811, and the baseball field all in earshot of the steamboat docks …

> Commodore JS Jones says the steam boatmen's baseball club awaits a challenge from the Accidentals …The Axes should not hesitate to take the river men in tow.
> *Daily Ark Gazette,* May 9, 1876

Baseball seemed the wholesome alternative to duels, but to some, a less than manly recreation. The *Gazette* periodically sniped at local baseball, from 1870, often from the un-named "little bald head man."

> Baseball is again a nuisance. Associated Press reporters think it very important that the public should be posted as to whether the Rip Snorters beat the Stunning Gushers or vice versa and send elaborate details of every game they can hear. As the baseballists have taken offense at our classing their little game as the national nuisance, we are impressed with the opinion that the *Gazette* will not be considered as the Little Rock baseball organ for this season.
> *Arkansas Gazette,* 1875

And, if little and bald, he was mean enough to invoke a dead infant at a time when infant mortality was all too commonplace. Notably, as of this writing, Arkansas infant deaths were commonplace occurrences, affecting 811 as well most families at least once.

> "To the parent whose son dies in infancy," says the *Louisville Courier Journal*, "there must be something peculiarly soothing in the thought of that, no matter what may be the fate of the child in the next world, it can never become a member of a baseball club in this."
> *Arkansas Gazette,* 1877

"No more baseball matches will be reported by the 'Little baldheaded man of the *Gazette*' unless he is furnished with necessary accommodation on the field. A table and chair is the idea. This is of interest to captains."
Gazette, September 1875

Bald, he could also be cryptic.

"Hot Springs is afflicted with the national game—base ball" "the little bald-headed 'man' that gets up our baseball reports I would suggest to Aunt Marie of this that her place is on the 'Homeplate' and they are she should 'hold her base' or she might possibly get forced out, Aunt Marie should be out in her little bed and rubbed down with half a dozen dead balls."
Arkansas Gazette, 1877

After a few years, the carping and outright cruelty of the little man just as suddenly stopped. One, or more, of the Accidentals might have changed his mind, with the help of a baseball bat.

The 1904 season was hampered by widespread rain plus a yellow fever outbreak and left the franchise deeply in debt. In 1905, with sportswriter purple prose that feared the very "future of baseball in LR was hanging in the balance," WP was a founding subscriber of a reorganized LR Baseball Association that kept minor league ball alive.

Serious ball was played at Association Park, adjacent to Jacobi Grove, a saloon, and a vineyard. Col. Zeb Ward, owner of The Farm before Feild Bros, leased the land and improvements, including fencing and grandstands, for $300 year ($8,000 in 2021) The Grove served as venue for a host of activities, secular (that included baseball) and sacred (including religious gatherings).

"...summer resort just been fitted up at heavy expenses, quiet pleasant, arbors and parlors for ladies and gentlemen,

and just the place for picnics. The best wines, liquors, lager,
beer, and cigars"
R Jacobson, prop
Daily Arkansas Gazette, March 19, 1876

Colored Farmers Convention
Our colored friends met in solemn conclave at JG yesterday
... whatever be their grievances they have no more to
contend against than their white neighbors.
Arkansas Gazette, June 1879

"Primitive baptists services"
Arkansas Gazette, March 1880

Baseball play shifted in 1901 to West End, and later to Kavanaugh Field at West End Park, now the site of LR Central High School.

With Jim Crow, recreation space in general, and baseball in particular, was segregated, so the Colored Sunday School Union bought 10 acres southwest of town at 36th and Potter. From 1905, Union Park provided a venue. The Civilian Conservation Corps added a recreational building in 1936.

Ernest's son Ernest Jr and daughter Eloise Feild Weir developed the EJ Feild Addition, adjacent to Feilds' Addition. On 10 acres there, the Lamar Porter Field, —I before E—Field, with a 1,500-seat grandstand, built by the WPA in 1936, operated to the present by the Boys Club.

In 1931, Traveler's Field provided grandstands, and lights from a Memphis ballpark were acquired and installed for night games. The park was renamed Ray Winder Field in 1966. Mr. Winder (1885–1967) started selling tickets in 1915, moving to business manager and finally part owner. In 2006, unable to bring the facilities up to League standards, the Travelers moved to Dickey Stephens Park in North Little Rock.

XIII.

URBAN

"We consider the underlying fallacy of the plaintiff's
argument ..., 'enforced separation of the two races
stamps the colored race with a badge of inferiority.' If
this be so, it is not by reason of anything found in the
act, but solely because the colored race chooses to put
that construction upon it."
Justice Brown for the majority

"Our Constitution is color-blind.... The law regards man as
man, and takes no account of his surroundings or of his
color when his civil rights as guaranteed by the supreme law
of the land are involved."
Justice Harlan, sole dissent
Plessey vs Ferguson, 1896

The telephones are running, and connection has been made.
Let them be used for business purposes and no nonsense.
When you talk to anyone, ask his name first.
Arkansas Democrat, October 1879

Mr. H.N. Stone arrived in the city yesterday from Memphis
where he has just completed the publication of a "Telephone

Directory and Railway Guide."... He will at once start to work
on a similar publication.
Arkansas Democrat, February 1881

Edward McGee, age 24, color black, personal property
$150, birth in Arkansas, can read yes, can write no, U.S.
citizen yes
Mattie McGee, age 23 wash and Iron, age 23, cannot read
or write, U.S. citizen
U.S. Census, 1870

The telegraph brought the world closer in 1861, as the closing
of the Arkansas River by war had made it more distant.
Southwestern Bell arrived in Little Rock first, but in 1879, 10 initial subscribers' telephones were all Western Union connections.
By 1893, the Southwestern Bell Directory listed 1,200 subscribers.

Two years later, the first electric lights were installed, Markham
on to Center and Main Streets. All nine customers were businesses,
five of them saloons. Power was on from sundown to 10 p.m., or
midnight for extra cost. Other competing electric suppliers arose.
Not until 1926 would there be a single power system for Little Rock.
The city bought power but operated the streetlights until 1958.

The 1862 Morrill Act Land Grant established two- and four-
year colleges. The sale of more than 10 million acres of indigenous
tribal lands provided funding. A second Morrill Act in 1890 allowed
funding for African Americans, but segregated schools. The
Arkansas Industrial University in Fayetteville opened with four faculty, seven male students, and one female student in 1871. WP,
Ernest, (and then after the name was changed to University of
Arkansas) Pappaw, Daddy, Mama, me and my siblings, and my son
each followed, as did football. The University established a segregated Branch Normal School in 1875. (later Arkansas Agricultural,
Mechanical and Normal College, University of Arkansas at Pine

Bluff) for training teachers. Arkansas Industrial University would become the University of Arkansas in 1901.

A Football Challenge

The University football team challenges any team in the state whose members are under the age of 21 to a game or series of games of football to be played at Little Rock, with a rugby ball, and under intercollegiate association rules.

Durand Whipple, Secretary

EE Breese, Manager

Arkansas Gazette, October 1888

I am an alumnus and faculty member of the University of Arkansas School of Medicine, now the University of Arkansas for Medical Sciences, College of Medicine. Readers will indulge me with some of the details. Nineteenth century medicine was actually a hodge podge of science, pseudoscience quakery, tradition, and, as is often the case today, luck. Hydropaths, naturopaths, homeopaths, electropaths, herbalists, patent medicine sellers, all manner of purported healers were in practice. Allopathic medicine would be the winner, the forerunner of current scientific medicine, emphasizing correct diagnosis and specific treatment.

A medical school opened in 1879 as Arkansas Industrial University on 113 W. Second Street, with $5,000, a six physician faculty, and 20 students housed in the former Sperindo Restaurant and Hotel. In 1908, Arkansas was one of the last six states to license doctors who had not attended medical school.

The school received no financial support from the state until 1911. Due to fear of competition with private practice, by law, the hospital operated as a charity facility until 1965. After 73 years, the first African American graduate, Edith Irby Jones, graduated in 1952.

Medical education was offered in a variety of venues and formats—almost all of it terrible. The allopathic American Medical

Association and Carnegie Foundation funded a national study, headed by Abraham Flexner, of the over 200 U.S. medical schools. The standards applied were a European model, two years in science classrooms, with laboratory training, then two years of supervised patient care. In 1910 The Flexner Report was published, a scathing blunt instrument:

Medical Department, University of Arkansas: Organized 1879. An independent institution, not even "affiliated" with the state university whose name it bears. Laboratory facilities: After an existence of thirty years without any laboratory facilities except a dissecting-room and a laboratory for inorganic chemistry, a frame building has recently been supplied with a meager equipment for the teaching of pathology and bacteriology. The session was, however, already well started and the new laboratory not yet in operation. No museum, no books, charts, models, etc., are provided. Clinical facilities: Hardly more than nominal.... The students see no contagious diseases; obstetrical work is precarious; of post-mortems there is no mention ...
Date of visit, November 1909.
General Considerations: Both the Arkansas schools* are local institutions in a state that has at this date three times as many doctors as it needs; neither has a single redeeming feature. It is incredible that the state university should permit its name to shelter one of them.
Abraham Flexner

*The other institution, the College of Physicians and Surgeons, was at least as poorly operated. Both schools fielded football teams and competed for the Sawbones Championship of Arkansas. In 1909, surpassing academic deficiencies on the field, the football team for the University Medical Department, the Medics, won a state championship 14-0 before a crowd of 500. They also fielded a baseball and lawn tennis team, and of course, a Glee Club.

Flexner was not impressed.

The medical school occupied the aging and increasingly decrepit Old State House from 1912 to 1935. The WPA built a real education facility, roughly where St. John's College stood, adjacent to City Hospital. In 1956, the current campus opened with probably the last un-air-conditioned hospital in the South. Relief from the heat was finally, blessedly, installed in 1966. The venting and blowers were sadly mounted at floor level, effectively decreasing each patient care room by more square feet than the already small rooms could readily accommodate. In the 1990s, Dr Tom Bruce, Dean during my matriculation, told me his biggest mistake was handing me my diploma in 1978. I think he was kidding.

Saw bone! Jaw bone!
Groan and yell!
M-e-d-i-c-a-l!
Quinine! Strychnine!
Stomach and jaw!
U. of A. Medics
Rah, rah, rah!

The Flexner Report and the changes it implemented did merge and close schools. All the programs around the U.S. that educated women physicians were immediately doomed due to already thin support. Schools graduating African American were affected, though some died a slow death. Today only two remain.

The Bros, ages 20-26 years in the 1880 Census. Town growth had slowed dramatically, only 800 souls over 10 years. It had been 20 years since Feild and Dolley had 150 gallons of hard spirits in stock, and now the Women's Christian Temperance Union meetings were at the home of Mrs. WP Feild, 811.

One new citizen added that year was Douglas MacArthur, who was born in January 1880 at the Arsenal Tower Building to Captain Arthur and Mrs. Mary Pinkney ("Pinky") MacArthur during the captain's yearlong assignment at the Barracks. Strolling, playing, or watching baseball, a Bro would tip his hat to pretty officers' wives, including one addressed as Mrs. Pinky, with her baby boy in a pram. General of the Army MacArthur viewed his place of birth as an accident, claiming Virginia as his home, while residing permanently in his suite at the Waldorf Astoria in NYC.

Feild Ernst J, clk Maxwell and Edmondson, bds 811 S Scott
Feild Joseph H, law student, 316 W Markham, bds 811
Field, William P, dep clk U S Court, bds 811
City Directory, 1880-1881

Joe read law, 1880–1881, with attorney JM Rose. There are no records that he was ever called to the bar, or referred to himself as an attorney. And in other matters legal, Rush's estate was finally settled by Silas, a mere 21 years after his death. The next year, the paper, with flourish, cited the 1653 book, *The Compleat Angler*. A fishing trip to the Saline River of Fisherman Ernest, with friends, made the news.

"Disciples of Izaak Walton"
Democrat, July 1882

Five months later, William "Presley," Jr, was born to WP and Florence at 811, and "Ar-Kan-Saw" not "AR-Kan-Sas" was finalized as the official State pronunciation. The French language fluency in the state General Assembly was not recorded.

Be it therefore resolved by both houses of the general assembly, that the only true pronunciation of the state, in the opinion of this body, is that named by the French from the native Indians and committed to writing in the French word representing the sound and it should be pronounced in three syllables with the final S silent, the 'a' in each syllable with the

Italian sound in the accent upon the final and last syllables,
being the pronunciation and now still most commonly used;
and the pronunciation of the accent on the second syllable
with the sound of "a" in man and the sounding of the terminal
"a" is an innovation to be discouraged.
Arkansas General Assembly, 1883

WANTED—a practical farmer who wishes to go to the
country and take charge of a hotel and farm in a pleasant
village. Address 811 Scott Street, Little Rock

A Little Rock Relief Association was formed by civic and business leaders. Charity supplicants initially appeared in Police Court to plead their case and undergo subsequent home visits by the police. January 1886, another approach was undertaken and provides a rare sighting of, and insight into, Uncle Joe, so I include this verbatim.

A GOOD RECORD ...

As Secretary ... I have the honor to report ... In order that all
applicants might have a hearing, daily ...at the police court
room..., Sundays excepted. A large number was in
attendance each day, and everyone thoroughly questioned.
The name and address of the applicant were taken, thorough
investigation was then made by some responsible person,
and no relief granted unless on a favorable report.... the
police at first performed this duty, ... they had to be relieved
from it and a person especially ... The services of JH Feild
were procured January 27, 1886, at $12 a week. He proved
to be energetic and faithful and eminently discriminating.
The daily sessions closed March 17, 1886, having been
extended over a period of eight weeks. A few have been
furnished relief since that time.... There has been disbursed
out of the fund $1,284.40. The above amount was

distributed in sums of $1, $2, and $3, and no duplicates under seven to 10 days. The applicant received no money but only checks made payable to some responsible grocery merchant, on which only the plainest provisions could be drawn. 439 of these checks were issued all of which were presented at the bank except four—two being returned and canceled, and the other two still outstanding. The following statement is as follows:

Amount distributed by 339 checks. $857.80
Amount for 91 cords of wood in half cord lots ...$319.50
Amount expended for railroad fare.....................$13.10
Amount paid to JH Field for services $94.00
Balance in treasury...$285.81
Total amount $1,570.21

Every effort was made to have a careful distribution of the fund and I can safely say that few mistakes were made.

Mr. CE Kidder volunteered his services.

WC Ratcliffe secretary

It was the unanimous opinion of all present that Judge Radcliffe discharged ... rare, good judgment and discretion. While no meritorious appeal for charity was denied or overlooked, none of the funds of the society were squandered on unprofessional deadbeats or other fraud. Treasurer of the Board, Mayor Boot acts as disbursing agent for the presenting grant temporary relief to such worthy objects of charity as may be brought to his attention.

Arkansas Gazette, May 1886

Uncle Joe, all of 26 years old, was found to be eminently dis-criminating in investigating his fellow citizens. Spouseless and childless, he assured that others with dependents were provided only the plainest provisions. He drew his salary out of the same funds as the needy, for part time work, four times what a needy case could receive. Mr. Kidder, also lauded, volunteered his time and talents, though what those were was not recorded.

Sanborn Fire Insurance Map of 1886 shows 811 and two out-buildings at the rear, one labeled "servant." The family, which had occupied the entire block, now shared it on either side, a 16-room boarding house to the north, a residence to the south. A stroll to the Arsenal and grounds entailed exiting the back gate, a short cut across Cumberland, Rock Street, and a Bro was there. Traffic would not be a danger for decades. The unreconstructed Silas lived at the corner from Scott Street at Ninth and Cumberland occupied the entire block.

The Little Rock Barracks were decommissioned in 1890, the land ceded to the city in a land swap and renamed Arsenal Park, though commonly known as City Park. German immigration to the U.S. peaked in the 1890s:

Wanted—Help
Wanted—good cook; German girl preferred.
Apply 811 Scott Street
Arkansas Gazette, February 1887

A fraulein could feel at home in Little Rock. At various times three German language newspapers—*Arkansas Staats Zeitung*, *Arkansas Frei Presse*, and the *Arkansas Echo*. The German National Bank had been opened in 1875, though the name would change during WWI to American National Bank. Sermons were preached in haupt Deutsche (High German) at the Lutheran Church, at Eighth and Rock, closer to 811 than First Church. The church began to offer Sunday night English language services in 1885, and even after WWI continued with special occasion haupt Deutsche services until 1940.

For the 1887 City Directory, the family self-described as plan-tering, managing farms, but living in town.

In 1888, Pappaw was born to WP and Florence at home at 811. Two years later, Pappaw's brother, "Little Harry" Harrington (1891–1893), made a brief sad appearance. Only three years before his cousin, identified only as Infant Feild on burial stone, was born at Silas's house around the corner. The postmortem portrait was a common remembrance at the time. A painting, still known to family as "Little Harry," showed a sweet faced, strawberry blond, smiling boy and made every other of my family uneasy. The pediatrician in me understands the perils of early childhood in the 19th century. With the macabre provenance, Harry now resides, safely in the Robert's Library collections, never to creep out a relative again.

Ernest married Jennie Clark (1869–1918) and purchased two properties in his name, for $200 and $1. They moved to the $1 home, which Will had previously bought on College Street. It was a bucolic setting on the town's southern edge. But a mid-1890s house fire led them to return to 811, and there they remained. Jennie was from Colorado, and their family traveled back and forth. The Bros' approach to a farm labor shortage was unenlightened:

Feild Bros plantation ... importing negroes from Louisiana
Daily Arkansas Gazette, 1896

Wanted—A white family to cultivate an upland farm on shares; good houses, water, and healthy location; references required.
Address WP FEILD, 811 Scott, Little Rock, Arkansas

Feild's Farm may have been as large as 1,800 acres. Acreage was always approximate as the river inexorably eroded the south bank, carrying farmland to the Mississippi River as silt.

In 1899, WP served as chair of the Mineral Products Committee at the Little Rock Board of Trade. At the time, Little Rock Cotton Gin, Quapaw Cotton Mills, Little Rock Oil (cottonseed oil), and Compress, and Little Rock Cotton Sheds were located along the Arkansas River and highlighted the economic importance of cotton. With no other local sources for minerals other than stone quarries, the importance of WP's office, and role of the Committee, is uncertain. Originally, the Little Rock Chamber of Commerce was founded in 1866 and located on East Markham in the Ditter Block. The group went through multiple iterations but was always pro-business, white, and male. First known as the Cotton Exchange in 1882, then followed by the Little Rock Cotton and Produce Exchange 1883, and the Little Rock Board of Trade in 1884, then back to the Little Rock Chamber of Commerce in 1914, then the Little Rock Board of Commerce in 1918, and changed yet again in 1924 to the Little Rock Chamber of Commerce. There were a multitude of mergers over decades, with Merchants, Association, Young Men's Bureau, Real Estate Bureau, Profitable Farming Bureau, Clearing House, State Fair Committee, River Transportation Bureau, and Industrial Development Committee.

In 1893, the boll weevil was found north of the Rio Grande for the first time. A conference to address the menace was held in Dallas. The Arkansas Cotton Dealers Association and Little Rock Board of Trade both sent delegations that included Ernest and the Mayor. The Convention generated a Proceedings Report that covered the sessions on planters, merchants, bankers, oil mills, and proposed legislation. The program demonstrated the shadow cast by King Cotton astride the South. No one addressed the farm workers or sharecroppers. The state finally eradicated the insect in 2005, but rural poverty remains.

XIV.

TROUBLE IN RIVER CITY

Between 11 and 12 o'clock last night a general row occurred
in Fighting Alley between citizens and soldiers. No weapons
were drawn, but fists and clubs were used. Police whistles
were sounded, and specials appeared, but as the soldiers
had the advantage of numbers, no arrests could be made.
Arkansas Gazette, 5 July 1874

Squatters' Island along the RR tracks between Lincoln Avenue
[now Cantrell] Viaduct and the Arkansas River is not actually
an island, but a stretch of river edge land which has been
taken over by about a dozen homeless families. The
inhabitants have thrown together shacks of scrap lumber and
tar paper. Tomatoes, okra and peppers thrive in the alluvial
soil. Pumpkin vines dangle over the bank and jackbeans
cover the sides of the cabins. When the River climbs toward
the cabins, about every three years, the squatters anchor
their shacks to the giant cotton woods, load their household
goods into rowboats, and row to higher ground. When the
flood recedes, they shovel the mud off.

Escaping inmates from the state penitentiary, now the Arkansas Capitol grounds, used Rose Bayou, also known as Penitentiary Bayou, as an escape route traveling upriver along the level bank or River Pike, then through the Feild Farm property.

Little Rock strived to be part of the New South, but a Bro walking north up Scott Street toward the river would pass segregated churches, Presbyterian and Christian on the left, Episcopalian on the right, white ladies of all ages on the left, the Young Ladies Seminary across the street, the Old Ladies Home for "white women … of unblemished moral character … respectable old ladies who have outlived their near relatives," and the "Chinese laundry." The future site of the Board of Trade was on the right. All upright and exemplary works and good deeds.

As transcontinental rail travel began, the Little Rock and Fort Smith Railroad laid their first 24 miles of track, and the first newspaper reference was made to "Fighting Alley." That square block on the riverfront was wide open, with saloons, prostitutes, and crime, including murders.

River News

The river will go dry if it keeps on falling. No arrivals or departures of steamboats, and business as usual as a matter of course dried up on the levee. Fighting Alley furnishes amusement for the wharf boat brigade in the interim.
Arkansas Gazette, May 1870

Residents were focusing on various entertainments. Fifteen-year-old WP played ball for the Actives, and lost to the City of Roses Team. Kate Merrick, madam and proprietor of the Ocean Wave Saloon in Fighting Alley, lost a different, most ancient of games, being denied a permit to enlarge her "house."

But there was more rowdiness than just yelling and screaming "Root, Root, Root" for baseball. There was real trouble for them what wanted it. Waiting at the northern terminus of Scott Street, Fighting Alley was every mother's worst fear. Also known as Battle Row and Hell's Half Acre, the block bounded by Wharf, Ferry, Water, and Elm streets offered saloons, dancing, and gambling. Newspapers never missed the opportunity to smirk, snicker, and then print "bagnio," a gentrified term for brothel borrowed from New Orleans, with a straight editorial face. Bagnio might be French vocabulary that some in the General Assembly did know.

DEAD FOR LESS THAN A DUCAT
A Stranger Stabbed to Death in Kate Merrick's Bagnio for Forty Cents.
Arkansas Gazette, September 1876

Men, women, cocks, dogs engaged in fights day and night. Fists, clubs, pistols, and artillery were used, and at least one Friday night card game was disputed. At Markham and Rock, a fight entered Gus's/Ellerman's Saloon from the back door, moved past the bar and among the patrons, and out the front. A stabbing followed on the sidewalk.

In one day, in March 1872, Miss Merrick and seven other "proprietors of *maisons de joie*" were rounded up and taken to court, fined, and released, but seemingly not reformed.

The City Jail, referred to in the papers as the "Calaboose," was on West Main (now Broadway) between 3rd and 4th Streets and was a common destination from the Alley.

Jennings ended the discussion by drawing a double-barreled shotgun on Rhodes who dashed from the saloon....
[Jennings] ran round the corner and found policeman Pryor,

with the gun still at his shoulder.... Proceeding to the 'boose,
Rhodes called Jennings vile names and was struck by
Jennings ... [Pryor] lodged both men in the calaboose.
Arkansas Gazette, July 1873

Nonviolent means were used as well. A singular, quasi-potable product, Fighting Alley Lightning, was sold and consumed, often to a sufficiently detrimental effect to garner mention in the next day's *Gazette*. In August, Kate was closed down until further notice, which must have ended by December, as two patrons filed complaints of having pockets picked.

One writer claimed it rivaled Natchez Under the Hill, though whether this was a snide brag, a fact, or a sentiment of genuine public shame was not clear. One of many civic attempts to clean up the area took "vagrant ladies" of the Alley and put them on display as a chain gang for street maintenance along Scott Street. Whether their work extended south to the 800 block of Scott Street was not recorded, but even the *Gazette* was moved to express shock at the spectacle made of women.

The Ocean Wave Saloon appeared most often in local news—fights, at least two murders, robberies, and swindles—from Union Occupation to the 1880s. "Miss" Kate Merrick was listed in a City Directory as "Madam"— not an honorific, but rather job description—as proprietress in an establishment of the world's oldest profession. In news articles, she needed no further introduction or description of her profession, nor did her staff, referred to simply as "the girls." Likewise, the Capital, the Arsenal, the Calaboose, the Ocean Wave, or Fighting Alley in a news article needed no description, address, or location. When one got "on a high" and "took in the elephant," the reading public needed no translation.

Joe McCollough, charged in attempting to kill Kate Carble, alias Kate Merrick, was examined before Magistrate Webster yesterday and honorably discharged.
Arkansas Gazette, February 1875

Mr. Carlos—not the Spanish Don of that name—was up in the police court yesterday morning charged with kicking up a shindy at a low dive in Fighting Alley. He raised a row because he had been charged $52 for a night for lodging, which was considered somewhat unreasonable, and Carlos was released. Two of the inmates of the house, Maggie West and Molly Milleheyser, were arrested upon the charge of robbing the don but in absence of sufficient proof were discharged.
Arkansas Gazette, July 1876

Besides Fighting Alley and Squatters Island another area of notoriety appeared in the press in the early 1900s.

"May Fox and Lizzie Spencer White were fined $500 and sent to six months at the county farm by police court. The specific charges against the women were disturbances of the peace. The precise offense was indecent conduct in the Swamp Poodle district."
Arkansas Democrat, August 1909

In 1913, the city made a concerted effort to shut down prostitution.

XV.
TWENTIETH CENTURY

Little Rock: The Most Prosperous and Progressive City
in the Southwest
Arkansas Democrat, January 1, 1900

ACT 104
AN ACT to require persons, companies, or corporations
operating streetcars to provide for the separate
accommodation of white and colored passengers ...
Acts of Arkansas, 1903

After one year from the ratification of this article the
manufacture, sale, or transportation of intoxicating liquors
within, the importation thereof into, or the exportation thereof
from the United States and all territory subject to the
jurisdiction thereof for beverage purposes is hereby
prohibited.
XVIII Amendment

The right of citizens of the United States to vote shall not be
denied or abridged by the United States or by any State on
account of sex
XIX Amendment

CONDUCTORS DID MUCH EXPLAINING
First Day of the New Streetcar Law
Fewer Negroes rode on the streetcars of Little Rock
yesterday than any day since the strike of two years ago,
when there was a boycott on the cars and they ran empty
all day long. The cause of this sudden determination to
walk was due to a law providing for separation of white
and Negro passengers on the streetcars. The Negroes
have organized a "We Walk" league, and at a recent
meeting there is said to have been a resolution adopted
providing that any member found riding on a streetcar
should be fined a stated sum, each ride to constitute a
separate offense. Those Negroes who did ride were
principally small carriers and women. It is estimated at less
than 10 percent of the usual number of Negroes
patronized the streetcars yesterday.
Arkansas Gazette, May 1908

All the trouble we have is from the whites and the
inconvenience of shifting seats.
JA Trawick, General Manager

The Civil War was long ended, XIII and XIV Amendments ratified, and separate but equal was the law of the land. Discrimination and segregation evolved to keep up with technology and infrastructure. Mule-drawn streetcars began service in 1877, Main to 17th Street, with 811 conveniently just off the middle of the route. Then came horse, mule, and new electric streetcars, and if one had the fare, they no longer walked or used a carriage.

Capital Street Ry. Co. Mainline 17 miles; owned two
horses, 308 mules, 42 cars, and five other vehicles. This
company succeeded, by purchase, April 1, 1890, the
Little Rock Street Railroad.

HG Allis, Pres.; George B Rose, Vice Pres.; HP Bradford,
Secretary, Treasurer and Superintendent.
General Office, Little Rock, Ark

City Electric Ry. Co. Mainline, 3 miles; steam motors 2; cars
14. Howard Adams, Pres.; WW Benjamin, Secretary; John B
Jones, Treasure; FJH Ricker, Supt.
General Office, Little Rock Ark.
Poor's Manual of Railroads, Volume 23

The car barn on North Street between Chester and Ringo, 100 yards long, was wide enough for eight parallel tracks. The dynamo power plant was adjacent.

The Bros were aware of the dawning of a new era in transportation. In 1902, Grandpa Hunter, who arrived in Arkansas mounted on a horse, departed life stepping off a streetcar, sans axe.

Levi Keys, in the town's first automobile, tooled around in his six-horsepower 1899 Model Woods Electric, made in Chicago.

By that year the second auto was on the streets—a 1900 Locomobile steamer. Horses and people had yet to encounter gasoline-powered transport.

AUTOMOBILE VS THE HORSE
Something About the Growth of the Automobile Habit
Fifty Machines Here
Pioneer cars were brought here a few years ago by Prof Levi
Keys and WC Faucette—accidents few.... The entire populace
turned out with one accord to the awkward-looking little
machine ... the police ... regard the "buzzwagons" as
harmless beasts.
Arkansas Democrat, June 1906

Mater's family's transition to the automobile is documented. There was a risk, uncommon, but very dramatic in using horse power. Conflagration was not uncommon, such that the editor gave it a two-sentence paragraph.

RH Mills' barn at 2124 Wolfe Street was burned at 8 o'clock yesterday evening with 4 tons of hay and other feed. The origin of the fire is unknown.
Arkansas Democrat, November 1905

Daddy, told stories to his grandson Stuart Mills Feild who recorded them:

[Around 1900–1910] my grandfather, my mother's father, Rufe Mills, was a local insurance man and dealt a little in real estate on the side. He had an office down on Markham Street, and he lived between 22nd and Wolf Street. It's a good long drive. On this occasion, he was riding in a buggy. He was driving, and with him was my grandmother's brother, Tom Salter. My grandfather was a very frugal man. He did not grow up rich and had to be careful with money, but he had bought a horse from the city that once had been a fire horse. It pulled horse-drawn fire engines. It obviously would be a good horse. [He] prided himself as a pretty good judge of horse flesh. But anyway, they were driving home, and all was going well until they happened to hear a fire engine with the "CLANG CLANG CLANG" of the bell that the fire engines used. Everything was going fine, and when the horse heard the fire engine, the horse followed the fire engine. Now this wouldn't have been so bad, but the fire was where the airport is now, which is a long way from downtown Little Rock and a long way from 22nd and Wolf Street. Now, where they were in their journey home I don't really know, but anyway, to go from somewhere on the road to 22nd and Wolfe is a long way from going to the airport. Well in spite of all the yelling and the shouting and the whipping and all my grandfather could do, the horse paid no attention and did what he was supposed to do, or thought he was, and simply followed the fire engine. Well, there was obviously nothing he could do but just go along for the ride. And to make it just that much worse, when he got to where the fire and all the excitement was, somebody hollered, "Here comes the chief." Which I don't think he thought was too funny, and after a ride he didn't want and probably was very, very, late for supper. End of story.

And after the fire, and the fire horse, my grandfather told me the story when I was a small child. I was probably eight or 10 years old, and he probably told it more than once. He worked for a short time for the Worthen Bank and Trust. Somewhere shortly before 1910 or maybe 1911 or 1912, among the other benefits, he had the privilege of a company car, a Model T Ford. My grandfather never learned effectively to drive, never owned one. He went to and from work, and when I was a child, he went on the streetcar, on public transportation, and on this occasion, he and another employee were making a business call, somewhere here in Little Rock in a residential area. As they were getting close, his companion asked him, "Rufe, are you going to turn at this next corner?" and my granddaddy said "I don't know. I'll have to wait until I get there."
Recorded by Stuart Mills Feild, circa 1995

With a streetcar junction at Ninth and Main, much of Little Rock was a three-block walk or less to a streetcar stop. Junctions and car stops, not parking lots, the town was still for people, not automobiles.

By 1910, a group traveling in four autos, made the run from Pine Bluff to Little Rock in only four hours.

A 1902 rare sighting of Joe with Ernest attending the Pine Bluff Fair led to a rumor in the news "that they [were] in the market for a Jefferson County farm."

In the new century, citing WP's role as U.S. Circuit Court Clerk, he was asked to "assist in collecting data on the Negro … gathering the data from his personal information as far as possible," for the Carnegie Institute volume *Economic and Industrial History of the United States*, specifically "The Negro in Slavery and Freedom." Unfortunately, the request came from Alfred H. Stone, a Mississippian working in DC with the Institute. In 1898,

> "he [Stone] rejected sharecropping and rented land to African American workers, refused to give credit or favors through the plantation store, and had complete control over day-to-day work."

Stone was surprised by the failure of this effort, and that surprise inspired his respect for sharecropping as a "kindly system of labor control." When Carnegie did publish in 1915, WP was not a listed source.

In 1902, the Arkansas Military Academy opened with WP on the Board and Executive Committee.

WP became a member of the Board of Mercantile Bank in Little Rock in 1902.

The Concordia Club, the first social club in town, was founded in 1864 by members of the Jewish community, two years before a congregation B'nai Israel was formed. The new club was built in 1903, at 801 Scott, replacing the existing 14-room boarding house.

> The new home of the Concordia Club on the southeast Corner of Eighth and Scott has been completed at a cost of about $35,000 and is one of the most complete and best appointed club homes in the country.... Concordia is about 39 years old and one of the oldest, strongest, and most influential social clubs in the South.
> *Arkansas Democrat*, June 1903

The club brought more status to the block and the town's social whirl to next door.

The structure was described as "magnificent" and "considered for many years the most elegant in town." Events of up to 400 guests would have made for a lively—and noisy—block. The club moved southwest of town, near the community of Douglasville, to a country club setting in 1923.

The household varied with marriages, births, deaths, domestic help, enslaved then freed. Pappaw told of 17 people seated at the dinner table. A description from Silas surely is similar. Water was supplied from "an old Indian well." Through the day, a fresh bucket was drawn hourly and placed on the back porch. Every meal "looked like a parade" with selections of meats and vegetables, three or four breads, all served to the family.

Everyone knew—and saw, heard, and smelled—everyone else's business. Open windows allowed shared indoor sounds and smells. Families kept poultry, dairy cattle, and horses, and dogs and cats wandered and multiplied. Each lot had a privy that was emptied more or less periodically—or into the water table. Wood and coal smoke from cooking and heating joined cooking smells. Indoor and outdoor noise of horses' hooves, creaking conveyances, peddlers, laughter, grief, anger, babies and children, marital and otherwise lovemaking, childbirth.

One 1903 Scott Street celebration was not held at the Concordia but next door.

Mr. William Hume Feild and Miss Mary Rebecca Jameson were married in Danville, Yell County, Arkansas, April 10, 1853, and on Friday last they celebrated the golden anniversary of that event at their home in this city. The Feild residence, 811 Scott Street, is one of the old landmarks of the town having been erected in 1840 and was formerly occupied by Mr. Feild's father, Judge Feild, of the State

Circuit Court, and in the old antebellum days was the center
of a generous hospitality, and the scene of many a brilliant
social gathering. Here, Mr. and Mrs. Feild reside,
surrounded by their children and grandchildren, who we
wish for them yet many happy returns of their wedding
anniversary. During the day, Mr. and Mrs. Feild were
recipients of hearty congratulations of a large circle of
friends and relatives, notably Mrs. Gilbert Knapp of this city,
only surviving sister of Mr. Feild.
Arkansas Gazette, April 1903

The article does not state that surrounded by all those many
family members was the norm, 24/7/365. A lot of people large and
small, but the U.S. Census included a Mr. Reeves, enumerated as
a servant, resident on the premises. His presence, and also a full-
time cook, lightened the load. The setting mentions the house as
a landmark, but also old, and the scene of brilliant events, but 40
years in the past.

It was not only the shifting currents and moving bank of the
river that affected Farm acreage. Jordan Bayou, the eastern downstream property boundary, a stream as small as a creek, generated
a legal dispute, with legal jargon to match, bigger than the actual
body of water.

The dirt track from the road to the river along the eastern border of the golf course today is 100 yards of wooded beauty along
the otherwise unseen Bayou.

WP served on the Board of Trade Minerals Committee, but
there is no record of his role in the eminent domain rights the
Legislature granted to mining interests. Bros sued the Arkansas
Railway Mining Company that same year to deny a rail spur and
right of way through the Farm and in 1905 won.

And WP had at least one frivolous moment in the public eye, organizing a smoker (a men only night out) for fellow movers and shakers.

On the motion of WP Feild, the Committee on Arrangements
was instructed to arrange for three speakers at the smoker.
Board of Trade, Finance and Entertainment Committees, 1903

If the speakers were actually more exotic entertainment, the secret is lost. If alcohol was involved, it was not discussed, in the newspaper or in the parlor of 811.

And another cryptic sighting, no details, and no notice was made of his return.

JH Feild left this morning for St. Louis, on business.
Arkansas Gazette, June 1898

A Pulaski County Fair Association was founded with "Feild Bros" among the stockholders, and Joe popped out of the shadows.

STOCKMEN TO MEET HERE TO ORGANIZE
Judge Asher Announces Important List of Delegates
to Meeting

The article proceeds to name dozens of male citizens, but among them, Uncle Joe was listed fourth.

Mary Eliza Feild Officer Knapp was the Bros aunt who breakfasted with guns and Bowie knives in 1845 and opined on the town's elegance. She did marry well, twice, and had an eye for elegance in husbands. She married husband William in 1848, and they bought farmland across the River, 16 miles downstream. With her second husband Gilbert Knapp, adjacent lands were acquired. The Indian Mounds, ascribed to Toltecs at the time, and the indigenous artifacts, were of interest to her. She made a detailed study, which was published in 1877 under her name, in the Annual Report of the Board of Regents of the Smithsonian Institute. Research has since found no connection to the Toltecs, but evidence suggests it was the site of a Quapaw settlement from 7th to 11th Century. Working with the Quapaw Nation, the State in 2022 renamed the area Plum Bayou Mounds Archeological State Park. In 1883, Mary Eliza contributed to local elegance by co-founding and naming The Aesthetic Club, a ladies' literary society. They met in homes, but in 1889 moved to the Arsenal Building in City Park, a stroll from 811. She died very well off in 1905 and singled out only Joe, not the other Bros, for a $500 inheritance ($14,500 in 2021). Her will included "three old servants," who received a less than generous $50 each for their long service.

The Bros appealed to the newly incorporated town of Pulaski Heights to annex the planned West Rock subdivision. Built and marketed as an addition for "colored" residents. The Bros protested, lest their property taxes go up, and they presented a petition opposed to annexation.

Some question was raised yesterday, also, as to the names signed to the petition...It was claimed a number of the signers were not qualified.
Arkansas Gazette, August 1905

The "not qualified" were African Americans, disenfranchised by Jim Crow.

Increasingly, the Bros were in local courts, over the Farm and what they viewed as encroachment. They had concern for the Farm watershed, at the top of the bluff above the railroad tracks.

The protest of the Feild Bros. against installation of a septic tank on the Little Rock College property [now St. John's

Seminary], near Forest Park was referred to the Board of
Health and Superintendent of Public Works.
Arkansas Gazette, September 1916

Will died at age 81 in 1908, Mary Rebecca the following year.
Family time and socializing were dictated by the weather, and
warm nights meant open windows, sitting outdoors on the porch
or the lawn, hoping for a breeze.

This story was told to me by my mother, one of the stories I
heard early when I was a small child. Her younger sister
Louise was ... a little bit of a spoiled child and she and her
other sisters, my mother and my aunt, used to go round and
round. Shortly after 1910, I think my aunt was probably 11 or
12 years old, it seems that probably one evening, when it
was getting close to sundown, and there were a lot of
shadows, and people were mainly in their yards visiting, it
was in the summertime, and the rest of the house of course.
would be vacant. The family was out, relaxing after the day's
work. My aunt was upstairs in their home on Wolfe Street.
They had a large old home there, and my aunt was upstairs,
and ... heard the wind blow a shade or a curtain and make a
noise that startled her to such an extent that she shouted, out
loud, "GOOD LORD BLOODY MURDER!" Well, this
aroused, of course, almost the entire neighborhood, she
shouted so loudly. And even one of the neighbors, after
hearing this noise, came charging into my grandparents'
yard, and house, with a revolver in his hand. Well, they went
upstairs, and nothing was ever found nor anybody. So, what
actually frightened my aunt, well, we will never know that. But
I think it gave her a pretty good scare, and gave the family a
pretty good laugh.
Daddy, recorded by Stuart Mills Feild.

As a small child, Louise's sisters and neighbors would refer to her as Teedles, which led to much wailing and gnashing of teeth. The story lived on of a housekeeper who begged, "Please! Please! Don't call Miss Louise Teedles." Yet as an adult, she was known to all family as Tookie, or Aunt Tookie to the kids, and was fine with that. Mater was always the full Mary Bernard.

And the Hillcrest neighborhood, where Aunt Kathleen and husband had built their house that Mater and Pappaw later acquired, and the same historic area where I live and raised my children, was marketed in ads as "what Scott Street has been in the past."

They continued in business as well as farming, Feild Bros reported in the news as investors in a fire insurance company and a cotton mill, and sold cotton seed anywhere from 130 bushels to sale by the ton. The Bros had bought, rented, and sold existing houses, but now became developers, Feilds' Addition, four square blocks in Stift Station. Unlike other developers, the canny Bros wasted nothing and claimed what they could, including …

> the right to use any dirt, timber, stone, or gravel from any of the streets or alleys, of said addition for purposes of filling, leveling or otherwise improving any of the lots, … claiming what others would have hauled away, further reserving all privileges of whatever character for the use of said streets and alleys for any other purpose, then for use, or as a highway for footmen and vehicles.

Block 7 judged ideal for a school, sold to Little Rock School District for Woodruff School for news reports of a "reasonable" $5,800 ($163,000 in 2021). Streetcar service was a boost for the new addition.

The Federal Courts Offices were reorganized, and WP saw his Clerk position abolished. He went full time into banking at Mercantile Trust and continued planter-ing. The bank was founded by local businessmen in 1902, with $250,000 stock and WP as secretary. By 1915, he was vice president, with a balance sheet tallying $1.36 million ($35 million in 2021). The company merged to form Union Mercantile Trust, which managed to survive the Depression and bank failures. Presley remained with his solid Federal salary and status as Deputy Clerk of the Federal District Court.

All United Daughters of the Confederacy will please remember the important meeting at Mrs. Mary Feild's Wednesday afternoon at 3 o'clock.
Arkansas Democrat, October 1899

The Daughters were instrumental in the Lost Cause myth of secession, and civil war was in full flower. In common terms, it was to preserve "our" (sic) happy way of life. The Cause held that the enslaved had been happy and loved their happy masters. The master took care of his slaves. The War had been about our state's rights, which then and now, were first and foremost the right to enslave those black happy folk. And anyway, the Yankees cheated. One of us was worth 10 of them. Robert E. Lee was a genius and a saint. We woulda, coulda, shoulda whupped 'em.

The United Confederate Veterans Reunion was on May 16, 1911, with WP on the organizing committee. The reunion drew more than 140,000 people, 12,000 veterans embraced by many Union veterans as well. No citizen could have missed encountering some part of it. Once again, 811 had a front row seat, the veteran tents and encampment around the corner at City Park/Arsenal grounds. Some Union veterans attended and were welcome. The African Americans who observed the hoopla had different experiences. Edward McGee's participation is unknown, doubtful as a celebrant, in spite of the service of his brothers.

African American women organized the National Association of Colored Women in 1896. The next year Charlotte Stephens, first local African American educator, set out organizing the Woman's Club, in 1905 as the Federation of Arkansas Negro Women, and then chartered in 1912 as the Arkansas Association of Colored Women, sharing the national motto, Lifting As We Climb. The white Arkansas Federation of Women's Clubs, voted to withdraw from the national organization of clubs if African American groups were admitted. In 1916, the AACW was included in the citywide "Clean Up, Paint up" event. Mentioned in upper case, women's groups listed after the male organizations. The Arkansas Association of Colored Women was only grudgingly mentioned, and then the single group accorded only lower case typeset.

Board of Commerce... Little Rock, Federation of Women's Clubs, School Improvement, Associations, Housewives league, Real Estate Bureau, negro, women's clubs
Arkansas Democrat, February 22, 1916

Colored Teachers State Association of Arkansas.
The first annual convention of the Colored Teachers State Association of Arkansas will be held in Little Rock, Arkansas, at Bethel ME church, corner Ninth and Broadway, Tuesday 14, Wednesday 15, and Thursday 16 June 1887. Every teacher and friend of education is requested to be present. All teachers and visitors to contemplate attending the association and desire the assistance of the executive committee in securing accommodation will please forward your name immediately to the committee.
Arkansas Democrat, June 1887

The Committee arranged for housing in private homes, Jim Crow preventing hotel accommodation. Like many of his rules, every reader of whatever race, knew this without further explanation.

Arkansas school children were exposed to indoctrination and race theory long before the current day.

Slave holders came with their slaves, opened large farms and plantations, and where a dense wilderness before, became a region of flourishing cotton fields. The masters protected and supported their slaves. The slaves obeyed and loved their masters. Better homes were built, and art, music and learning began to exercise their powers over the people.

The History Of Arkansas, A Textbook For High Schools, Public Schools, And Academies
Josiah Hazen Shinn, 1905, pages 112–113

Mater's maternal grandfather, Richard Salter, was listed in the 1860 Census in New Orleans, occupation: Gentleman. He owned a large plantation across the Mississippi, commercial and residential properties, a shipyard, and drydocks. In the southern tradition she went by "Mary Bernard," Bernard being the maiden name of her maternal grandmother. She was known by the double-barrel name socially and among family for her entire life.

Not yet a Feild or Mater, she graduated from Little Rock High School in 1912 with her Normal Certification, which allowed teaching lower elementary grades without a college degree. The Colored Teachers State Association of Arkansas notwithstanding, Mater never taught alongside any African American colleagues, nor taught any African American students. Mater taught in the Little Rock School District until 1960. Her 48-year career was topped by Charlotte Stephens, founder of the local affiliate of the National Association of Colored Women. She began teaching in 1869, age 15, until she retired 70 years later.

Little Rock School District's policy paid Mater's colleagues less than white colleagues.

Much later, in 1942, Sue Cowan Williams, teaching at Dunbar Junior High, objected to the fact that African American teachers and principals were by matter of practice paid less than white colleagues. She filed suit in Federal court, lost, and then won on appeal. The School Board committed group perjury, in straight faced performances.

> All the individual members of the Board of Directors were called as witnesses in this case, and each testified they knew nothing of a salary schedule, had never followed one in fixing salaries, and had never instructed the superintendent to follow one in recommending salaries.
> MORRIs v WILLIAMS et al.
> Civil Action No. 555. District Court, E. D. Arkansas, W.
> January 5, 1944

> "She is colored, a person of African descent, and of Negro blood;... that defendants, over a long period of years, have consistently pursued and maintained a policy, custom, and usage of paying colored teachers and principals less salary than white teachers."

> "that the question of race and color never enters into and has never entered into his consideration of the salary to be paid the applicant or teacher; that he has always been aware of the race and color, but he has only considered the value. The Superintendent has testified at length, and on extended questioning by the plaintiff on cross-examination, and by defendants on direct, he has stated positively and unequivocally of the individual to the system in the position he had to fill."
> Little Rock School District

She was fired, along with her principal, who though male, was the President of the African American City Teachers Association of Little Rock. In 1952, she was reinstated, though she was asked by the District Superintendent "if she had learned her lesson." She taught at Dunbar until 1974.

The Central Arkansas Library System was integrated in 1957. The Branch library building adjacent to Dunbar was named in her memory in 1997. She had died in 1994.

World War I, or the Great War, began as Germany swept the low countries and France, and cotton was 12¢/pound. Fifty-two years after

> "Mr. Thomas Johnson had told me the War was to set the colored people free. I believed him and felt if it was so, it made me feel pretty proud. I wanted the Union cause to succeed. Yes, sir."

Edward McGee, still driving but still working for someone else, was listed in the 1915 City Directory as "Driver GG Wood Coal Co." The Federals he had proudly anticipated arrived. He had not anticipated they would leave and that Jim Crow would arrive and set up shop. He rightly expected emancipation would mean freedom.

The Bros and the Farm played a role, albeit for profit rather than high mindedness, in the end of Pulaski County contract convict labor, a brutal, and often times corrupt system in the South. Convicts were leased to citizens. At the state level, contract labor ended in 1912. Advertised as frugality, in practice financial starvation, the General Assembly did not appropriate enough funds to operate a state farm large enough. So, the governor paroled enough convicts so that the remainder would fit. Locally, the solution was that the Farm property was leased for convicts to work. Certainly, hogs thrived there, and there was plenty of work for mules.

Judge Asher Leases Feild Planation
Further leasing of the county convicts will come to a stop....
(Asher) signed a 3-year lease for a 700-acre plantation ...
where all women (and) ... men not able for roadwork and...
able bodied to handle farm machinery about 600 acres ...

suitable for cultivation ... (under a) share crop plan. The
owners WP, EJ, and JH Feild will act the part of farm
operators, but all control of convicts will be reserved by the
county officials. A big stockade will be built and all sanitary
arrangement will be used in the handling of the prisoners.
Arkansas Democrat, March 1912

Buckets and the river bank sufficed for sanitary arrangements.

Pappaw and Presley registered for the World War I draft in the
waning four months of the war. In addition to advanced age of 30
years, Pappaw had a deferment as essential farmer, and Presley, even
older, for good measure listed "hard of hearing." The war almost
over, The Bros managed to anger the U.S. Army and infuriate their
fellow city fathers. They refused, whether by a vote of 2–1, or 3–0,
a U.S. Army offer of $1000/acre for 55 acres, (one million dollars
in 2021, now the site of the Bill and Hillary Clinton Airport).

The securing of the big enterprise was made possible by 50
Little Rock businessmen, who gave the government a
guarantee that it would be able to secure the desired site for
$1000 an acre. The owners, the three Feild brothers, have
held out for $1500 an acre. Court proceedings will be
resorted to, and the local businessmen are guaranteeing that
if the price fixed by the court is more than $1000 an acre
they will make good the difference.
Arkansas Gazette, July 1918

Four days later

Is Announced That Papers Have Been Served Upon Feild Bros
Major Howell, Judge Advocate at Camp Pike, announced that
he had served papers requisitioning land for the site of the
army aviation warehouse upon WP, JH, and EF Feild, owners

The facility was budgeted at $1 million, and the asking cost $82,500 ($2 million in 2023). Fifty members of the board of commerce initially pledged to pay the Army the difference, but later reneged. It was ruled that the Bros would be paid cost, determined by appraisers, and the land requisitioned.

The Farm Ledger volume 1918–1923 lists 48 individuals, and the 1919 cotton price was 32¢/ pound.

The Bros did serve the war effort and arranged for what would be the only sustainable cash product—but from under the Farm, not on it.

WATER COMPANY TO DRILL WELLS
Arkansaw Water Company announced the company had let a
contract for the sinking of three additional wells in the vicinity
of the present ones…. The new wells are to be sunk on what
is known as the Feild property.
Arkansas Democrat, September 1918

Later, the properties had been sliced and diced, equitably on paper, but there had been no practical way to be fair. The tangible asset divided truly equally was liquid … water.

PULASKI CHANCERY COURT FINAL DECREE
The division was made subject to the Contract with the
Arkansas Water Co., dated August 31st, 1918 … and rental
during the term of the lease we hereby equally divide…
July 19, 1923

Farm sharecroppers received food and supplies from the Farm, charged against their earnings from crop sales. Prices from the ledger for basic commodities seem generally in line with the area. The commissary ledger records, in Pappaw's handwriting, show accurate basic addition, subtraction, and honest prices in general. This is a low bar of sound business, but was historically lacking in many owners' dealing with sharecroppers. Typical basic items were salt pork, coffee, sugar, tobacco, soap, lard. The Farm was located close enough to town that perhaps Sherrill's Store in West Rock, the closest, and other competition within walking distance, held prices in line. Pappaw would sometimes underwrite purchases from Sherrill. However, as price of cotton rose and fell, the final tally of cumulative debt of shares, and Farm income can not be determined.

Many entries started with a "Cotton pkg," $46.51 in 1918, seed, tools, and incidentals. Farm families could rent "corn land" at $12.50 an acre every season, also raising pigs, chickens, vegetables. There were also Pappaw's notes to Sherrill's Store in West Rock to extend credit to individuals. There were also handwritten transactions, sometimes on scrap paper, including this four-way transaction, involving a father, son, Pappaw, and Mr. Sherrill. One entry for $30 for funeral expenses to Will Saunders's account. The total Ledger accounts total over $10,000. The Farm traded with local businesses beyond Sherrill's. In March 1919, Reinman and Wolfort, on Seventh Street, sold to Fields (sic) Bros two mules for $450.

In 1920, Cooper-Dickinson Grocer Co, invoiced Feild Bros $94.07 for merchandise including Brown Mule chewing tobacco. In 1921, Chas. F. Penzel Grocer Co. a receipt for a sale to "RH Fields (sic)/(delivery by) wagon" and "Ross, wagon repair." There are 1920 bills to Feild Bros for services of Dr. E. O. Day and Dr. E. E. Johnston, 700½ South Main, for several Farm families, including medicines, the men as well as family. Johnston listed both a home and office telephone, Day neither. E. O. and wife were, for the purpose of birthday parties and silly hats, among the crème de le crème of local medics.

The Farm was mentioned in at least one crime story.

Albert, Gus and Nathan Randall, Negroes, who have been wanted for a week on charges of assault with intent to kill Charles Robinson, another Negro, were arrested this morning on the Feild plantation west of Little Rock by Deputy Sheriff George Rising and James Drake. They furnished the bond to appear Saturday afternoon in Municipal Court for preliminary examination. The three were wanted in connection with an attack on Robin Robinson about a week ago. It was thought for a time he was fatally hurt. He was treated in the City Hospital.
Arkansas Democrat, April 21, 1915

Families included Wyatt, Callaway, Threet, Williams, and Bailey families in Farm records. Ms. Lois Threet's oral history notes that her future in-laws

"moved to West Rock from up on Feilds' Farm."
Oral History, Roberts Library

About 88 percent of West Rock residents were related to one another. The West Rock neighborhood had their adjoining homes and businesses and housed the CO&G Depot. W. S. Holt was the developer of the neighborhood, and he advertised

"We are selling to colored people and have no hesitancy in saying that of all the good things we have sold to that class of patrons, this is the best."

The African Americans from the Farm and West Rock were educated at Pilgrim Rest School, Pulaski Heights Road. The first recorded listing of Little Rock School District schools was in 1910. In October 1914, Pilgrim Rest School had enrolled 14 students.

In addition to Pilgrim Rest, there was Riverside, which was located near Cantrell Road. Riverside was specifically for African American students and was first mentioned in School Board minutes in August 1914. Mrs. Josephine Pankey was the first principal. She went on to be a very successful major land developer locally. She went to bat against Jim Crow loan practices.

"On the strength of Mrs. Pankey's endorsement, the bank made a number of loans to young men who otherwise would not have qualified for a loan. If the borrower didn't pay the note to the bank, I would call Mrs. Pankey. Sometimes she would ask us to give the borrower more time, if he had a good excuse, such as illness or unemployment."
Aubrey Williams, 1991 letter:

The Red Summer, or Red Scare, of 1919 led to violence across the U.S. With cotton prices at an all-time high, the Elaine Massacre in Phillips County occurred. The total number killed never determined. If mentioned, it was the Elaine Race Riot, described as a violent uprising by local sharecroppers. Grif Stockley's book and scholarship by UALR Dr. Brian Mitchell disabused the state of the myth, recognizing the Elaine Massacre. That same year, the Volstead Act brought prohibition, though the family, except perhaps Presley and his fast crowd, being teetotal.

Little Rock is the Financial Commercial, Industrial, Social, and Political Center of the nation's most progressive state.
Arkansas Democrat, January 8, 1921 (page 6)

A landmark during Federal Occupation, 811 in 1920 was 80 years old. It would have been drab, drafty, heated poorly for an age of natural gas that was installed around town starting in 1911. Electricity, gas, and plumbing, both in and out of the house, retrofitted. The multistory, modern, brick Concordia Club was next door, handsome, but looming over the north side of 811. Large, beautiful homes had been built around it, Queen Anne and Italianate architecture. And in the newer neighborhoods, with population increases, electrification of the streetcars in 1891, and then automobiles, location and walking distances were less important.

In older years, WP seemed the more staid Bro, reflecting his role in the U.S. Courthouse and later as a bank officer. During Florence's final illness with TB, they had relocated to the house at 476 Ridgeway that daughter, Kathleen and her husband Edward Tobey had built, with a live-in cook and helper in the frame servants' house, 476 ½ Ridgeway, in the backyard. When the Tobeys moved to Memphis, Pappaw and Mater moved in to a home that was constructed with installed electricity, gas heat, hot water, and indoor plumbing. The modern conveniences were not enjoyed for long. Florence died December 28, 1920 of tuberculosis. WP would not return from Memphis to 811. Ernest traveled more than the others, with Jennie's family in Colorado. Uncle Joe ever the quietest, his last newspaper mention was 1911. Property taxes were reduced, Feild Farm going from $10,720 to $8,160 ($130,000 to $90,000 in 2020 dollars).

Cotton fell, or more accurately crashed, from 36 cents a pound, to 8 to16 cents. On May 8, 1921, WP died, then on May 23, Joe died. Joe's 1918 will specified his share of jointly held property for four charities, requiring liquidation by the estate. Lawsuits by family filed against Joe's estate. Last Bro standing, Ernest and family were living at 811 when the final entry posted to the Farm Commissary Ledger on October 27, 1923.

XVI.

THE END, ALMOST

Pappaw did what he could with his third of a third. He tried to hold as much farmland as he could, but he was tied to an anchor already on the way down to the bottom. King Cotton equaled sustenance.

When Cotton Is High
You hear some laymen say that they do not blame the
farmers for planting all cotton when the price is so high.
Passing over the indisputable fact that there can be no
guarantee that the price will stay high, let us bear in mind
what Bradford Knapp, the Department of Agriculture's Chief
of Extension work in the southern states, said at a meeting, at
which the Second Arkansas Profitable Farming Campaign
was launched, the government figures prove that a bale of
cotton at $.18 a pound will buy no more food at the present
time, and in some instances not so much, as would $.12
cotton in 1915. And suppose the price of cotton should not
be high as the price of food for man and beast should be.
Or suppose the farmer's cotton crop should be a failure and
he would have to pay high prices for all the food he used
for his own household and his stock?

Will, then the Bros, then Pappaw stuck with cotton. And land. For all the Progressive and New South talk about manufacturing and diversification in the local economy, they stuck—cotton, and the land it grew on, underpinning the value of their financials, as well as other institutions they were involved with. From 1865 when war shortages raised prices eight-fold, prices then fluctuated widely through the end of the 19th century. Cotton had done well, but not to last. The Bros were current, or a half step, or 50 years behind the times. Persnickety cotton plants, and even more fickle world markets had the final say.

As has been characteristic of raw materials prices, the price of cotton rose and fell much more violently in this period under review than did the prices of all farm products. Cotton prices, as was previously pointed out, rose 468 percent between November 15, 1914, and April 1920, whereas all farm commodities ... rose 142 percent in the same period. The decline in cotton prices that ensued in the depression of 1921 carried them 75 percent below the 1920 peak level, while the prices of all farm commodities fell 52 percent in that depression.
The St. Louis Federal Reserve

Little Rock, the capital of Arkansas, is set like a Gem in the center of the Wonder State. Her citizens are energetic and progressive. Her financial institutions are in the hands of safe conservative businessmen.
Arkansas Democrat, January 1921

XVII.

THE END FOR THE BROS

In 1924, Ernest died in Crossett, Arkansas, from a ruptured appendix. His third of the estate went into local residential property.

Son Ernest, Jr., and daughter Eloise weathered the worst, developing E. J. Feild Addition, adjoining the western boundary of Feilds Addition, Stift Station.

In three years, the bulk of farm acreage sold, and generations of land ownership ended. But it had been over for a while, for Pappaw was listed in the City Directories 1925–28 as "farmer," "plumbing salesman," and "salesman" for Davis-Prieur, wholesale produce. Selling pipe and wholesale fruit and vegetables was a long fall from two sections of land, bales of cotton, hundreds of hogs, and tons of cotton seed.

Daddy was six, and 811 was knocked down, but across the road at 800 Scott, Floella McDonald, a 12-year-old, was found murdered in the bell tower of First Presbyterian Church. She was white. John Carter, an African American man was seized from the jail, lynched by hanging, his body burned in the intersection of Ninth and Broadway. No Atticus Finch, with his rocking chair and reading lamp, were on the steps of the calaboose, no sheriff in front of the mob, with a faithful deputy behind, racking their double-barrel shotguns, "ya'll had your fun, now go on home." Fathers took sons downtown, to watch the show. The macabre event drew a carnival atmosphere crowd. Papaw was disgusted and told Daddy so.

A family friend told of her Little Rock Police Department officer father and others receiving calls the night before telling them to stay home. And they did. Later, Lonnie Dixon, age 17, provided a dubious confession, was tried and convicted for Floella's murder by a jury that deliberated 12 minutes. He was executed just weeks later. Carter was innocent for certain, and Dixon was convicted without evidence. For the African American community, the message was clear. There was no protection from the law, or from the mob, for any male of the wrong skin coloring. And in 1929 with the Great Depression, Arkansas banks began to fail, ultimately a total of 66.

XVIII.

MAMA

Living on Ridgeway, Pappaw and Mater lived a life of the glass well less than half full, and ever fearful the contents were dwindling fast. Meanwhile, in contrast, Roy T. Edwards, Grandaddy (1895–1969), my maternal grandfather, felt he lived like a millionaire, believed that a half full cup runneth over. His great-grandfather, Hayden Edwards (1810–1887), was born in Shelby, Kentucky, and family had arrived in White County, Arkansas, well before Rush, in 1836. Life was scratch dirt subsistence farming, along with a small cash crop, cotton. My great-great-grandfather William F. Edwards, a Confederate soldier, enslaved no one, competed with the economics of slavery, reaping no benefits. A subsistence farmer, he was assessed and paid a County Confederate War Tax. He was wounded in the Battle of Helena and taken prisoner July 1863 and paroled from Camden, Arkansas. He paid the ultimate price, and died, either while walking toward home, or soon after return.

Granddaddy never had a chance for much schooling; the farm came first. Many Arkansas schools were on so-called split terms, of an already short school year. Classes halted in fall for harvesting, and spring for planting. A report card survives, one quarter cut by the teacher from a sheet of cheap notebook paper, handwritten and recording a total of 7 days attendance out of twenty-four. His low grade in arithmetic, was belied later with a consummate salesman's mental math, and memory of how much was ordered, by which store, on which day, at what price, his commission for cans, cases, and once, an entire boxcar of coffee.

Grandaddy married Christina (1900–1985), called Neenie by grandchildren, when she was 16. Her folks were Albert, German, pronunciation All-bert. Her mother's family were Wares, who moved from Kentucky to the Bald Knob area, maybe just ahead of debt collectors. The story my mama told varied.

Mama often spent the summers in Bald Knob, which was full of cousins. When there, kids did not wear shoes, except to church. All the Feilds wore shoes, all the time. In Bald Knob the generator ran from sunset to around 9:00 p.m., excepting Wednesdays. That was wash day, done by hand, in a washpot. The new electric iron was a rare household labor-saving device. At her maternal grandparents' farm, after supper, often the only light was the glow of the fire, whereas 811 was well lit, and 476 was wired as it was built.

In the 1960s, Roy and Christina recorded an oral history of a 1922 "vacation" in a 20-horsepower Model T, with one-year-old Mama, her three-year-old sister, and Roy's 16-year-old brother, Dale.

Roy: Back when we got married (1916), people didn't take vacations. Well, I guess the millionaires did, but we've never seen a millionaire. [Note: Billionaires, however, were later acquaintances—Granddaddy with Folger wholesale, and Christina with Sam and Helen Walton, pre-Wal-Mart.]

After a while, Christina and I got to where we made a dollar or two more a month than average. We decided to take us a vacation. Well, we actually called it a tour. Up to the Ozarks. So, we had a new Ford. Oh, it might have been a month or two old, but it didn't have a thousand miles on it. There were nowhere to go. So, we started. The old doctor, we lived next door to a doctor, fixed Christina up cough medicine, croup medicine, diarrhea medicine, chills and fever, he just give Christina a cigar box full of medicine. He [the doctor] didn't want us to go. Oh, we had hand (powered) everything—lanterns, axes, pumps. [Model Ts had a hand-crank starter until 1927-crf]. I remember that the ol' boy had a big ol' horse trough there in that pasture, so I just got in that horse trough and had me a bath. I don't know how Christina made it. That night the dogs got our food, so we started out foodless. I don't remember about the breakfast, how we handled that. We got through that day, but the next day we drove hard, and we got to Jasper the next day, that wouldn't be over 60 miles on state highway 7. And by that time, the brakes had gone out. New car you know. Ford had clutch bands. To put the brakes on, the clutch just clamped over the cylinders, and that stopped the car. There's this blacksmith shop there, and he knew how to replace them. We stayed all night there.

So the next day then we got to Harrison. Only 20 miles, but we was pretty wore out at that time. So, we camped in the park there at Harrison. We just stayed one night in Harrison. In the next day it was about 50 miles to Eureka. We were just wore out, because that was hard work, and (decided) to find us an apartment (since) Eureka Springs was a resort. A car like we was traveling in, you can't lock your stuff up. If you went anywhere, I mean you couldn't gone to the picture show (five years later the first talking motion picture was released—crf), so if you wasn't in your car and you wasn't in your tent, there just wasn't any way of taking care of them. The old gal, she come to the door she look up, and see those two babies and she said oh no, I can't keep those kids. No no, she just slammed the door. They were 2 and 4 [years old]. So finally I told one old gal, don't you just have someplace out back where we can just tie 'em up?

Mrs Fuller saw the two babies and she says, "Oh, I sure wants to see those babies. I sure have got a place for you." We wore the tires out. Tires just gone, four or five flats by then. I owned a garage [in Bald Knob], so I wired the old boy I left in charge to ship me a set of tires by express. It took about three days to get there.

Next day by hard driving, we got to Siloam Springs. They said we couldn't get to Fayetteville; the road was just cluttered with wrecked cars. And by that time, we'd run out of money. I knew the undertaker because he come from Bald Knob up here, to get a check cashed. I found his place but, he gone to do a funeral in Siloam Springs. Well, we struck out, and we met this great big hearse coming. Course, he knew me, grew up in Bald Knob. But he didn't have any money, jerked both pockets out. He says, "I'll write you a note to the undertaker in Siloam. He will take your check."

I remember we run out of purt' nearly anything to cook with. We bought a sack of apples, and we had fried apples for breakfast. It was awful good. It was pretty modern. They had a campground, but it was a community kitchen, build a fire, and cook what you wanted.

Kind of a roof over it. I think it had running water, And everybody (in Siloam Springs) was kind of suspicious of everybody because they just robbed the bank. [September 1922, five men attempted to rob First National Bank of Eureka Springs. Three were killed, the other two captured.— crf] We got into Fort Smith, found a park, and the first natural gas we ever saw. The park was piped with natural gas. You could put up your tent right by a little gas deal. I

guess somebody showed us how to light it. And next day we
drove all day and until about 2 AM, to get into Little Rock
from Fort Smith

And I don't know how many flats, the tires was a wore out
again. We just had one spare. You couldn't get five miles
sometimes without a flat, the dust was hub deep, just had to
get out there in the middle the night and patch a tire. Gosh!
And that took another whole day to get from Little Rock to
Bald Knob. I had a jack, but you patched your own tires. You
took the tire off and you prys it off with a tire tool and inflate
it with a hand pump. But we didn't need any of that
medicine! One of the kids threw her shoes away, we don't
know when, she threw 'em out of the car. All we found was a
little strip (paved) between Conway and going into Little
Rock. But that's all the paved roads there were on that trip.
Just some gravel here and there.

Tires, it was gone, car was worn out too. I don't remember
what we done with that car. Probably painted it, worked it
over, and junked it. I probably sold it for $75. You could buy
a new one for $390 or $400.. Neenie said "Oh! I wouldn't
have taken a million dollars for that trip!"

Some time later, Granddaddy and family scraped and saved
$1,300, planning to buy a small grocery. With a bank failure, that
money was gone, overnight. Over the next few years, Grandaddy
moved, with grocery chains, and wholesale foods, including
Uneeda Biscuits. The home electricity and the gas were intermit-
tently shut off, and with him on the road, the family huddled in
the back as creditors banged on the door. Grandaddy landed with
Folger Coffee and thrived. He called on country stores on dirt
roads, lit only by two or three dangling bare bulbs, and the growing
number of supermarkets. When laid low by rheumatic fever,

Folgers carried him until he could work. He sold enough coffee that Folger sent him to a World Series game In New York, making him the first forbear to fly. During WWII, he hired ROTC students to put on the uniform and ride with him to get around gas rationing. He attended some of the same civic groups that Sam Walton attended and took us grandkids to the Ben Franklin Five and Dime, Walton's pre-Walmart, a few blocks from his home. Neenie knew Mrs. Walton as Helen. Granddaddy had sporadically attended school. All four of his children attended college, one a Phi Beta Kappa, and Mama, a master's degree. The size of the glass and just how full is a very relative thing.

XIX.
AND MORE DEPRESSION

The stock market crash compared to the agricultural collapse and banks failing was mostly an afterthought in Little Rock. Pappaw's next-door neighbor had moved from the north and prospered, complete with chauffer that later drove Daddy and neighbor John to school. Presley, off to college in Tennessee in 1902, dropped out and his education finished. "Presley Feild, son of United States Circuit Clerk W. P. Feild, arrived home yesterday from Spring Hill Tenn., where he had attended college. He has been forced to quit his studies on account of trouble with his eyes." His trouble may have been failure to put his eyes on a textbook or inside a classroom.

Or maybe it was his eyes. Or he strayed from Temperance. "And members of the Party" reads more like the Society Page than a police report. Presley had stayed with his federal position, as Chief Deputy Clerk of District Court, on Colonial Court, behind Ridgeway. His Federal salary insulated him from Pappaw's and others' financial woes. But in 1932, his vision problem that had ended his college education did not impair his aim. He died of a self-inflicted gunshot to the head in the upstairs bathroom after the call from downstairs to breakfast. Descendants of both WP and

Ernest were told of his lifestyle—Cadillacs, automobile trips up north, such as an

"extended trip north, Chicago…boat to Milwaukee,
Waukesha, WI, 'Saratoga of the West'"
(*Arkansas Gazette*, 1917),

And Mary, his wife

"spending several weeks at the Majestic Hotel"
(*Arkansas Gazette*, October 1918).

And a

"Motor trip which included St. Louis, Chicago, Detroit, and
Memphis"
(*Arkansas Democrat*, 1922).

He and Mary adopted an infant. Just before, they spent weeks at Hot Springs and the spa town of Waukesha, Wisconsin, taking the baths. Presley had fathered a love child with their housekeeper, the story through both the WP and Ernest sides of the family. He embezzled funds from the U.S. District Court that supported his family and lifestyle. Discovery, or imminent discovery, was the cause of his death. In our family, his name was not spoken until after Mater's death.

Funeral services for William Presley Feild, who died Monday
morning, will be held at the First ME-South, Eighth and
Center Street, at 2:30 Wednesday afternoon with the William
Cem Reeves in charge. The body will be removed at nine
Wednesday morning to the home at 321 Colonial Court.
Arkansas Gazette, February 1932

Pallbearers were two first cousins, a judge, the dean of school, and attorneys and businessmen. That does not support the family story of scandal, at least in the immediate aftermath. As with his Uncle Joe's decisions on his will, no one will ever know for certain.

EX DEPUTY COURT CLERK ENDS LIFE
Presley Feild Despondent as a Result of Long Illness William Presley Feild, age 48, until recently chief deputy United States district clerk, ended his life at 8:30 AM yesterday at his house, 321 Colonial Court, by firing a pistol bullet into his head. Mr. Feild's resignation as chief deputy clerk was announced Saturday by government official, effective as of November 3, 1931. Members of the family told Dr. Young, deputy coroner, that a pistol shot was heard immediately after Mr. Feild had been called for breakfast. The body was in a bathroom on the second floor with a bullet hole in the right temple. A 32-caliber pistol lay nearby. The verdict of suicide was returned by Dr. Young. Dr. Morgan Smith, close friend of Mr. Feild and his physician for many years, said last night that Mr. Feild's health has been failing rapidly starting last August. Mr. Feild was worried to such an extent about his physical condition that he was unable to work and had been advised by Dr. Smith to resign many weeks ago. In November Mr. Feild went to the Mayo Clinic but returned without noticeable improvement. Lately he had become very melancholy and despondent, Dr. Smith said.

In 1944, three years into World War II, cotton finally regained the 1920 price. After the Farm failed, Pappaw was an employee, in a variety of sales jobs. At age 17, he had worked for Crane and Co, multistate wholesale plumbing supply. By 1933, he was back in the business and gradually was successful. Thirty-two years after loss of the Farm, he was President of the Plumber's Supply Company wholesale, on East Second Street.

XX.
DADDY, ME, ETC.

Daddy attended Pulaski Heights Elementary and Junior High Schools around the corner from 476. Mater did not like to drive, a good thing, as she was terrible at it. By age 12, Daddy was driving her on errands, though he was not allowed to go to Boy Scout Summer Camp on the Saline River. Mater was convinced his older brother Russel Jr. had contracted malaria there. She was not an alarmist. Through the 1920–30s Arkansas frequently led the nation in malaria deaths.

Lack of funds limited Daddy's education, after Little Rock High School, to an associate's degree at Little Rock Junior College. He participated in fraternity life and did not have to work. With a four-year college graduation rate of seven percent, that was a laudable achievement

On graduation, he worked as a bank teller. Rejected by the Army for a large hernia, he, with Mater's financial help, had the surgery done. By that time, no volunteers were accepted, the draft being used to fill ranks. Called up, he went willingly. He bitterly endured basic training at Camp Gruber in Oklahoma. That soured him on nature and the entire outdoors such that he declined every opportunity to camp when we were Scouts, stating he slept enough on the ground in basic. Except for one night at Boy Scout Camp Quapaw. There were not enough adults, and he had to take a turn. He showed his distaste by showing up, directly from work, in a sports coat, tie, and wing tips, and headed out first thing the next day. He did manage to avoid malaria. Though eager to join, certain of the cause, and no different than any other GI, he later took the whole exercise as a personal affront. He tried out as an Air Corps gunner, but failed the vision requirement. This may have saved his life, and made mine possible. Air Corps loses were higher than any other branch of the Army. He also had a brief assignment to the Rainbow Division which had a large casualty count. With his Associates of Arts degree, banking experience, and interest in the Air Corps, he was incongruously placed in administration in the Medical Corps. He was detached, with a small unit headed by a young physician, to accompany troops in transit to Europe on civilian ships. He shared a stateroom, but it was stripped to steel deck plates and bulkheads, bunks and lockers welded in place. He had 4 crossings, including the luxury ocean liners Queen Mary and Mauritania, and learned to hate curried mutton the ships' cooks prepared for the British merchant sailors. On a Christmas Eve, a horrific attempt at a spinal tap by the doctor in rough seas, was followed by death of a young soldier with highly contagious meningitis. To prevent panic among the 16,000 U.S. soldiers on board, he was part of a clandestine midnight burial at sea. The nightmares, that resulted were an annual part of his holidays, to the end of his life. Though he was never in combat, he heard depth charges from Navy escort ships fired at suspected U-boats, and a V-1 buzz bomb overhead, while in London. The overwhelming might of the United States was noticeable without seeing direct combat. He was able to be a tourist soldier, seeing Glasgow, Robert Burns Cottage, London, and even a trip to Paris. He noted from the train Cherbourg to Paris, the rails were lined by an uninterrupted border of wrecked and burned out, horse drawn and motorized vehicles, buildings, and mangled, dead, livestock. He was housed in a girls' school, with long lines of cots provided. The Army photographers took momento photos of soldiers 100 or more at a time, in front of the Trocadero, and managed to get 8x12 prints to each GI later.

He detested MPs for cruel and arbitrary violence. He resented officers, with the exception of physicians, as he was a two-year college man, with a repaired hernia. He had dislike of Army nurses in general, as they were officers, but he had a romance with an RN lieutenant from Brooklyn, who wrote he looked "Van Heflin." On VE day, he did not kiss any nurses in Times Square, as he was across the Hudson, wrestling drunks at a New Jersey Army hospital. In another story, he was assigned to guard German POWs. He was issued a broom handle, due to a shortage of police batons. He was discharged at the rank of Sergeant. The GI Joe experience was not for him. However, the GI Bill shaped his life and thus mine. After the war he went to the University of Arkansas Law School on the GI Bill. He lived in a rooming house, four men to a room. Like many, he wore the GI uniform, dyed to civilian colors and like others, was mocked by 18-year-old frat boys. He still managed to send cash home to Mater every month out of his laundry allowance.

It was harder for others. The legislature had funded tuition for African American students to attend graduate school out of state, if a program was not available at Arkansas Agricultural, Mechanical and Normal College. However, the university of Missouri had lost one such case, and two were pending in Texas and Oklahoma.

Silas Hunt, a WWII combat veteran and Student Body President at Arkansas Agricultural, Mechanical and Normal College. After a professor finished a class, he would teach the same subject to Hunt individually. Hunt could borrow books from the law library only through an intermediary... in a separate study room rather than space within the library...

He could not use the student restrooms but had to ask permission of the Dean's secretary to use the Dean's facilities.

The Dean was non plussed with another concern,

"he pleaded with us to try and find housing in the colored community and not saddle the University with the problem ... As they left the dean's office, they were subjected to some "curious stares" from students, but there were others who "venture[d] out and [shook] hands and offer[ed] a word of encouragement."

Soon

"Hunt had been joined in his separate classroom by white students who wanted ...more individualized attention from professors. The post-World War II class was filled with returning veterans who wanted to get on with their lives. They did not care that they were sitting in the same room with an African American."
Arkansas Historical Quarterly
Summer 2009

Daddy met Mama on a Halloween blind date. They moved to Little Rock, were married in the home of the Methodist Bishop. He went to work at the Little Rock office of a national insurance company as a claims adjuster and stayed until he retired. Not long after law school, but never having practiced, he briefly considering enlisting during the Korean War—as an officer—in the Judge Advocate Corps. He never did use his degree. Mama paid his Bar License every year. Growing up in the teetotal household, I was baffled by the term Bar. It sounded not quite right. The Women's Christian Temperance Union in the parlor at 811 would have been pleased.

Mama taught home economics. Just before I was born in May 1953, they moved to Pine Valley Road in a post-war subdivision, then west Little Rock. They raised three of us, my brother David born in 1954 and sister Jean in 1957. Two out of three houses had an ex-GI dad, and a nuclear family of two to three kids. No divorces, most moms were at home. Daddy was active in a social organization, the Y's Men's Club of the YMCA. With Mama, he attended an international conference in Banff, Canada. Like Pappaw and Granddaddy Mills, he was a 32-degree Scottish Rite Mason. He volunteered in the Civil Defense Auxiliary Police, called out on occasion to look for elderly persons who had wandered. But by the time I started elementary school, he largely stuck to home, other than church where he was an usher and thoughtful adult Sunday school teacher, and the occasional events with Mama, Scouts or PTA meetings. In high school, I played on a Boy's Club flag football team with friends. We were the only team in the league with an African American player, our friend Kenny. Daddy watched our game at Lamar Porter Field on the way home from work. Our opponents began with racial insults. They were very surprised when a man, in his tie and wing tips, charged across the field yelling "that's enough of that." He was friendly, but I do not remember a friend visiting him at the house. A neighbor who had been interned by the Japanese from Pearl Harbor to VJ day was more isolated, only comfortable sitting outdoors, in a lawn chair, alone in the middle of the lawn, and no walls. I think the depression that affected Mater and Pappaw struck him, albeit they were all high functioning. Presley as well may have been depressed, or was depressed by embezzlement, or depression led him to embezzle. The one positive of Daddy's later dementia was a brightened mood and money concerns melting away.

In 1957 four laws were passed by the general assembly act 83 through act 86. Governor Faubus signed into law four bills previously approved by a majority vote of Arkansans in a General Election:

Act 83 – created a State Sovereignty Commission, to investigated those supporting integration, including specifically the NAACP

Act 84 – relieved school children of compulsory attendance in integrated public schools

Act 85 – required persons involved in civil rights organizations and activities to register with and make periodic reports to Sovereignty Commission

Act 86 – authorized school districts to employ legal counsel to oppose integration

After a family history with the African American community from enslavement, through sharecropping and Jim Crow, Pappaw and Daddy were opponents of the 1957 Central High scandal. This was more related to the primacy of the law than support of integration, but also their prejudice against certain white folks, specifically white trash. There was no exact Feild definition of white trash, but it included sideburns, women with peroxide-bleached hair, cars parked on lawns, general coarseness, and the ultimate depravity, men on a front porch drinking beer in an undershirt. At that time, tattoos got a pass as they were usually associated with military service.

They strongly disliked Faubus, to the extent that even though I did not know what that was, I knew it was bad. Pappaw said of politicians, "they all sleep in the same dung heap." So-called leaders they detested included Jimmy Karam, businessman, preacher, and president of the Capital Citizens Council; preacher James Wesley Prudent; attorneys Jim Johnson and Amis Guthridge; the physician Dale Alford; and their rabble that surrounded the school. Pappaw did not allow the N word, though he would refer to African American men as George. The term dated from the use of "George" to address African American train porters, from George Pullman and his Railroad Sleeping Car Company, the company town of Pullman, and his vicious strike-breaking tactics. With Mama and Daddy, Pappaw drove his young grandchildren, lest we forget, past Central High School and 101 Airborne paratroopers, seemingly 10 feet tall to a child, at parade rest with fixed bayonets. That is my earliest certain childhood memory, and I am grateful.

In 1958, in a "by golly we'll show 'em" with acts of fear, defiance, ignorance, nihilism, and hate, all Little Rock high schools were closed. The following year, Mama joined the Women's Emergency Committee to Open Our Schools, a self-described group. The WEC was made up of white women, African Americans excluded after inclusion in early meetings led to white attendees walking out. But the segs were removed from the school board at the polls. In the STOP movement—Stop This Outrageous Purge—the 45 "pro-integration" educators slated for firing were retained, and the high schools reopened in 1959. The short-lived private seg T.J. Raney High School, after providing mediocre instruction, closed. It would be followed later by all-white private and religious Christian schools, and white flight to surrounding school districts.

In 1959, The West Rock community was displaced by urban renewal/removal. Eighty-three families were displaced, their homes flattened. Ms. Lois Threet, who has Farm memories, was the only African American employee of the Housing Authority. She had the sad role of notifying relatives and neighbors that what they thought was their thriving neighborhood was a slum. In 1961, 25 African American students desegregated the junior high schools. Ms. Threet's daughter Diane, who grew up in West Rock, was one of the integrating students at Westside Junior High School.

Mama did not drive. Thanks to that and to the city bus service, which stopped at our front door, I had transport, and a diverse racial and ecumenical exposure. Monday through Friday, as many as a dozen maids, housekeepers, and child-minders would get off the bus in the morning and depart in the afternoon. When I was young, most were dressed in white livery, head to toe. It was affable; depending on time and weather, my folks would sometimes shuttle riders to another part of the route, making their jouney home 20–30 minutes faster. Toward downtown, the bus stop at St. Mary's School for Girls and Convent was busy, and not just students. The nuns did not drive, and never went off campus alone, traveling at least in pairs. Doctor, dentist, shopping, public library, and sundry other nun business, in full traditional habits, head to toe. St. John's Seminary, three blocks from the close-by shopping area, the Heights, enrolled young men, easy to spot in black trousers, shirt, and white clerical collars. Saturdays seminarians were free, carrying white laundry bags over their shoulders to Banner Cleaners, and on return, picked up a load clean. And home delivery did not start with Amazon. Milk was from a dairy now the site of a Lexus dealership, eggs from a local man were delivered out of a station wagon. Fruits and vegetables were sold from the slow driving back of pickups. Purchases downtown need not be carried home on the bus. The Delivery Service, with a fleet of trucks, fanned out around 5 pm, bringing the day's shopping to the door.

Across the street, three sisters, two of them hearing impaired, taught at a school for the deaf. American Sign Language basics were part of neigboring. My elementary school had a significant Jewish enrollment. Every year of elementary school, there were Jewish classmates. By our kid standards, they were lucky, off for Jewish holidays, and the boys were out early once a week for Hebrew lessons. And Chanukah meant eight days of gifts in December versus one for us. So, there were many requests, to our Gentile parents, to become Jewish.

The Ninth Street community begun around a refuge for Freed persons, thrived then dwindled, in light of impending Urban Renewal removal. A branch of a local bakery chain was across the street from the Gem movie theater. On Saturdays, all goods were marked half price at exactly 12 noon. Mama struck up a relationship with the shop ladies, who would sometimes set back something nice for her. I ate bakery, not Wonder bread. We were the only white family on Ninth awaiting the bargains. Or for any reason. I was aware of the seeming exotic differences of the street and life passing by. Ninth Street was not exotic, rather, we were white.

I assumed every kid daily had a dozen African Americans (but only ladies, not men nor children) dressed in white out the front door, always went to and from downtown with nuns, saw young men carrying large white bags on their shoulders and horsing around in clerical gear, wanted to be Jewish, and shopped on Ninth Street. Around age 10, I first met an African American peer at a Cub Scout event where I heard a friend whisper an epithet that to that date I had never heard. I asked about it when I got home and was told to never use that word again. I knew Baptists went to Church on Wednesday nights, did not dance, or play cards. Based on his grandfather Mills' Know Nothing teachings, my dad feared Catholics obeyed the Pope's every command, and that the streets on Christmas Eve were filled with drunken papists on their way to midnight mass.

I rode a conveyor belt to success, with the other white sons, of two college graduate parents, living in a home backed by the GI Bill. I was accepted by Hendrix College, without an interview or campus visit. I would have had a National Merit scholarship, but Daddy and Mama did not even apply. They believed we did not need it; they would make it work. I received unexpected admission to medical school after my junior year, not even graduating college. I had taken the medical school admissions exam for practice. The Admissions Dean saw my scores and called me to 'strongly' urge me to apply. The first day of the first clinical year, I was assigned in-patient pediatrics. I went home and phoned Daddy; I knew my life's work. I trained in the U.S. and then London. Thanks to the infinite patience, and wisdom, of mentors, I had a reasonably successful, very satisfying, academic practice at Arkansas Children's

Hospital. I had fun every single day and was, amazingly, paid well for it. I fell in love at first sight, proposed on a third date, and have been wed 44 years. In the name of full disclosure, she turned me down approximately 400 times before acquiescing after two years, from either good sense or exhaustion. We raised two great kids to adulthood. I never really even had to plan. I had chosen my Baby Boomer parents wisely.

By the time *Fun with Dick and Jane* came along at school, every child in the South could read two other words: "WHITE" and "COLORED." Those signs in Little Rock, on every drinking fountain, restroom, entrances to public buildings, were finally removed by law in 1965, 110 years after WP's birth and a year before I finally attended an integrated junior high. I met an African American friend in seventh grade, one of 12 African American students in a student body of 700. Now, 38 private schools operate in Little Rock. The African American enrollment in the Little Rock School District is 79 percent, 15 percent in the private schools. The Little Rock School Board was dissolved by the state in 2014, replaced by a political appointee trained as an electrical engineer who had termed out of the Arkansas Senate. He then fired the District's most successful Superintendent in decades, perhaps ever. In 2020, with no measurable change in outcomes, governance was returned to the voters and the school board. As of 2022, the state funds competition to public schools.

In 1965, construction began on Murray Lock and Dam. The Farm, "Feild Bros, 476 Ridgeway," remained as the last 7.8 acres of the 1,400 acres, and a property tax burden. This last bit of the farm was at the south end of the original property, above the railroad. The tract was long, narrow, inaccessible, and at the top edge of a steep slope, effectively perpendicular. On the deaths of Pappaw and Mater, it was sold to the Country Club of Little Rock in 1968 and remains undeveloped.

In 1969, Pappaw died from advanced dementia, months after Mater, from congestive heart failure. The western half of the Farm was repurposed in 1972 when Murray Park was approved.

On November 6, 1992, the largest crowd in Little Rock since the 1911 Confederate Reunion, gathered at the Old State House for Bill Clinton's presidential election. In 1892, the crowd would have been heard all the way to 811. In 1998, Red's Pool Hall, the last business open on Ninth Street closed and the building demolished.

Great-grandchildren of WP are 21st century graduates of Central High. Pappaw, it turns out, was the family's one and only varsity football player.

XXI.

LEGACY, LOOSE ENDS

The Ridgeway house second mortgages finally were paid off in the1950s. The Great Depression for much of Arkansas began the day after cotton peaked at 476, never ended. Mater enunciated the letter "R" sparingly if at all when speaking, even in her own name, Mary Bernard/ Mah-y Behn-ehd. She spoke Deep South rather than Arkie twang, as did Tookie. She had continued to receive a salary as a schoolteacher, but refused to put money into the farm. They lost the farm, barely kept the house, and never shared a bed after that. Even after Pappaw was ultimately success-ful in wholesale plumbing, their lifestyle became shabby. He was president of the Plumbers Supply Company, an achievement that surpassed the bank VP WP managed. He and Mater both consid-ered him a failed planter. And that is how they lived out their self-inflicted shabby, genteel lifestyle.

Identified in City Directory and Census was High Germany: Hezekiah Jermany, from Stamps. A handy man at the Mills' Wolfe Street home, he was as tall as he appears. WWI draft registration lists him as 6 feet 2 inches. He was the most traveled part of the household. He was indeed drafted, traveled to France in the Army, arriving as the Armistice was declared, and returned.

(Col), i.e., African American, address listed as in the "rear" of 2124 Wolfe, with the careless spelling of African American names found in the newspapers and city directories. Hezekiah then moved to 476 1/2 Ridgeway, residing in the servant's quarters for some time. This was a 10 x 10 structure with gingerbread trim, and a front porch, a toilet was in the adjoining garage.

Then, Philander Smith College male students lived in the servant's house. They cooked and cared for the yard in exchange for housing and board. The students walked to campus for lack of carfare.

Neither the Feild nor Mills mothers, nor grandmothers, nor great-grandmothers, nor great-great-grandmothers had ever cooked, cleaned, or mended. Child-rearing had been at their direction by the enslaved in the home, and later paid domestic women. During the Depression, men would turn up at the 476 back door, as happened up and down the street and across the country, asking for work and food. None were denied at least something to eat.

Mater and Pappaw continued as teetotalers and turned in on themselves. Other than church ladies, there were no formal or even organized entertaining, not even family, in contrast to the 1910 front yard gathering at 811, and the evening on Wolfe Street when Tookie roused the neighbors to an armed response. As much as sports was a part of his early life, I never attended a Traveler baseball game with Pappaw. Daddy did tell me Pappaw had been offered a spot in the minor leagues in his youth.

We attended the First Church Christmas pageant and the Annual Picnic with them. That was the family year calendar.

Grandaddy Mills and wife Anna moved to Ridgeway for a time. Anna's grandfather, Richard Salter, listed occupation on the U.S. Census, "gentleman." How she and Mater navigated the modern world is not recorded, though they survived. Grandaddy Mills died in 1952 and missed greeting me into the world the next year. By the time my recollections begin in the late 1950s, the almost bare kitchen held a refrigerator with a broken latch, held closed by a kitchen chair leaned against it. There were few pots, pans, or dishes, and those were mismatched and battered.

In the dining room, there was a hole in the floorboard for the buzzer for Pappaw to press with his foot to summon the next course or have the previous removed. Beside the dining table and chairs, there was a massive oak sideboard containing wedding china and family silver, solid, not sterling, not plate, along with fine linens. The walk-in pantry, built large enough for household help to sit down and take their meals away from the family, was bare. They wore frayed clothes, washed by hand in the sink, hung to dry on the screened-in porch. There was never a washing machine in the house. Toothpaste was squeezed then the tube cut open, and soap slivers saved and pressed together so as not to waste. The TV bought for them was never switched on; their radio was from the 1920s.

They did take in a myriad of stray dogs—"Judy," beagle, inter-alia. Also, an occasional stray cat. The final one, after the aged, massive cat Old Gray passed on, was "Buck," who smelled bad and only barely tolerated Pappaw, snarling and snapping at the rest of the world. Late in life, Pappaw was bit on the hand by a stray cat Mater took in that suddenly decided to decline Pappaw's hospitality. When the hand turned massively swollen, red, and painful, she "doctored it" with turpentine to avoid a doctor's bill. When the doctor was finally consulted, beyond the antibiotic, he asked who the President was (Johnson). Pappaw did not remember. The last president he could name was Warren Harding. He could still throw a baseball hard and hit a long fly ball out of my front yard that was never found. Advancing dementia was hidden for a while by the empty lives they lived. At her death, gifts of clothing from Christmases and birthdays, were found open but never worn. Her classroom materials were under her bed, at the ready to start a new school year, and were there when she died. The frugality included no structural repairs, and little upkeep. The house sold for $13,000 the same cost as Daddy and Mama's 1,000 square feet in the Kingwood baby boom subdivision four weeks before my birth in 1953.

Time took a toll. The garage had burned long ago.

It was not replaced.

Mama for three or four years had the domestic services of Eula Mae, of whom I have warm, but nonspecific recollections. When I asked much later, she could not remember her last name. And for even more support for domestic tasks and parenting, she told of pills her doctor prescribed for energy and pills to sleep. In fact, she was taking dextro-amphetamine and Miltown/meprobamate tranquilizer. She saw the Beatles on Ed Sullivan in 1964, but missed the irony, declaring them to be "dopers." She benignly described a D&C Surgery (dilatation and curettage) as the response for ladies with missed periods—in fact a surgical abortion.

Big hugs were part of Mama's family experience, not Daddy's, though Mater and Pappaw were kindly. Their Little Rock grandchildren, who lived three-and-a-half miles away, never spent a single night under their roof. I ate a total of one meal there, of pot roast—one meal. At holidays, Mater would volunteer to bring green beans, which meant she arrived with canned beans, one can in each hand. Sold by their estate in 1969, the house later fell into further disrepair, along with the 10x12 "servants house" at 476½ Ridgeway in the rear on the alley. It had been the Field Bros' library, for neighbor boys, then empty, then for storage, finally hidden by vines with a sapling through a hole in the roof. The 476 foundation buckled; the roofs of both buildings rotted and leaked. The servant's house partially collapsed. In 2005, the house was beyond hope, demolished and replaced. Pappaw's practice of tipping wait staff in increments of a quarter, was continued by Daddy.

Joe's bequests had been indeed well placed for long-term public good. The Ada Thompson Home funds and residents were moved to Presbyterian Village retirement home in 1976, supporting the last surviving lady until 1991. Mama spent four dwindling years of non-indigent dementia at the Village, well cared for. The Methodist Orphanage became the Methodist Children's Home, then Methodist Family Health, with a building, the Joseph Feild Cottage, extant. When I was growing up, the Florence Crittenton Home became the Florence Crittenton Home for Unwed Mothers. Any question a child asked during annual church funds and canned goods collections about an "unwed mother" got a "HUSH" and poke from an adult elbow. The facility has operated since 2004 by Free Will Baptist Ministries as an emergency shelter for young people, pregnant teens, and mothers with babies. Uncle Joe, the Methodist baptismal sprinkler, might be appalled, the legacy in the hands of Baptist immersion dunkers. Hendrix College continues, affiliated with the United Methodist Church. A few First Church congregants survive who were young members of First ME Church–South, before reunification in 1939.

West Rock remained through the 1921 agriculture market fail, the 1927 Great Flood, and the Great Depression. There was opposition from residents and some support from citizens in the city, but Urban Renewal removal prevailed. The last mention of Riverside School by the Little Rock School District is the 1948–49 school year. Their spiritual center, the Pilgrim Rest Baptist Church, resettled on Confederate Boulevard. In 2015 Confederate Boulevard was finally renamed Springer Boulevard. Dr Worthie Springer was a long-time African American physician. His former clinic is now the Springer Building, on the Children's Hospital campus. It continues to house medical student and pediatric resident teaching.

The Chamber of Commerce and business community accepted, if not embraced, that desegregation or integration were not just the law of the land, but accomplished fact in town. In 1963 the business community offered gradual change, as in gradual after Emancipation, 13th, 14th Amendments, Brown vs Board, Central High 1957. They yielded to an opening up.

...the business community provided leadership when the general public was reluctant to accept necessary changes and when politicians were in thrall to the electoral benefits of supporting segregation. Pragmatic self-interest drove their actions, as they realized that a more progressive social and racial climate were absolutely essential preconditions for economic advancement.

Professor John Kirk, *Arkansas Times*, September 5, 2013

When the time came, many leaders' money was invested in private, re-segregated schools. Currently, the Governor and General Assembly direct State tax revenues directly to many re-segregated private schools.

XXII.

BLESS OUR HEARTS

These stories arrive at present day 2024, but do not end. My grandchildren may read this many years from now. There has been change. Things are better.

Each financial panic and depression took a toll on the economy. Every family, everywhere, everytime, 1837–Rush, Will–1874, Pappaw–1919, Grandaddy–1929. The boom/bust cycles are no more predictable or rare, but thus far there has always been a recovery, more so for some, and sooner for some than others. Childhood death took Feild children—Henrietta in 1833, Emma in 1858, Silas Leo in 1864, Little Harry in 1893, the Edwards' Virginia in 1874, and Claud in 1905, and the most, the Alberts' Eunice in 1892, Bessie in 1894, Charles in 1897, Lilie in 1900, Jonie in 1901, and Eulah in 1908. This vastly improved, by improved sanitation, nutrition, immunizations, and access to women's health care. Pediatricians, including this one, played a role. A large discrepancy in outcomes remains.

What was the Farm still floods, but erosion is stabilized. Downstream, where enslaved people loaded cotton, raised by enslaved families, there is a Presidential Library. Little Rock has an African American Mayor. First Church has a beloved African

American female pastor. She cast a vote with the 95 percent majority at the United Methodist General Conference to acknowledge and embrace our LGBT neighbors. A grandson is growing up in the now very diverse Little Rock Central High School Historic Neighborhood. Our son bought a house on the previous site of the School for the Blind, now the Governor's Mansion District, amongst diverse neighbors. In between, the Mills home on Wolfe Street is being restored as this is written. A historical marker will mark the West Rock community.

Things are different, but this work is intended to emphasize the need to strive for ever better. By many, this is derisively labeled as indoctrinated, woke, or snowflake. In fact, time and again, the truth shows that what seemed inevitable at the time was instead often a bad choice. The academic Critical Race Theory posits, that from John Pedro in 1619, enslavement, the local and national history of Jim Crow, and discrimination, to this day, are part of the national fabric. Governor Sarah Huckabee Sanders joins the ranks of leaders who failed the irony test and signed the Executive Order To Prohibit Indoctrination And Critical Race Theory In Schools.

"(CRT) is antithetical to the traditional American values of neutrality, equality, and fairness. It emphasizes skin color as a person's primary characteristic, thereby resurrecting segregationist values, which America has fought so hard to reject." At the close she doubled down, on faith, as well as race, noting the date as "in the year of our Lord 2023."

From blissful lack of awareness of entitlement, folks have devolved, smugly, brazenly to certainty they are entitled to their entitlements.

I have a sense of the multitude of roads traveled by my forbears and relations, to get me here. I found family trees misleading. They only seem linear, instead there are twists, loose ends, and dead ends galore. The roadsides along the way are too often not pretty.

I hoped to understand who I am and learn why I am here. Well, that was hubris, but yet, here I am.

In closing, some quotations from past and present:

"the War was to set the colored people free. I believed him and felt if it was so, it made me feel pretty proud."

"She is to choose between being the weakest of the 'Cotton Confederacy' and without hope of ever being stronger"

"Regnant Populus, The People Rule"

"Land of Opportunity"

"Ya'll aren't from around here, are ya'll?"

"Thank God for Mississippi."

"Go Hogs"

Lastly, I add,
"Bless our hearts."
Amen

Charles Robert Feild, May 14, 2024

ABOUT THE AUTHOR

Charles Feild is a paternal and maternal sixth generation Arkansas native and a pediatrician, by professional training. He enjoys history and storytelling, with an eye and ear for irony. He is married to Christina, from Glasgow, Scotland, with her own gift for history and stories. They have two accomplished adult children and an eighth-generation grandson.

www.ingramcontent.com/pod-product-compliance
Lightning Source LLC
Chambersburg PA
CBHW031256090426
42742CB00007B/476